The Art & Making of ARTHUR CHRISTMAS

AN INSIDE LOOK AT BEHIND-THE-SCENES ARTWORK WITH FILMMAKER COMMENTARY

Aardman & Sony Pictures Animation

Edited by Linda Sunshine   Designed by Timothy Shaner

NEWMARKET PRESS
NEW YORK

TM & © 2011 Sony Pictures Animation, Inc. All rights reserved.

This book is published simultaneously in the United States of America and in Canada. All rights reserved. This book may not be reproduced, in whole or in part, in any form, without written permission. Inquiries should be emailed to permissions@newmarketpress.com or write to Permissions Department, Newmarket Press, 18 East 48th Street, New York, NY 10017; FAX (212) 832-3629.

FIRST EDITION
10 9 8 7 6 5 4 3 2 1

ISBN: 978-1-55704-997-1 (hardcover)

Library of Congress Catalog-in-Publication Data available upon request.

QUANTITY PURCHASES

Companies, professional groups, clubs, and other organizations may qualify for special terms when ordering quantities of this title. For information, email sales@newmarketpress.com or write to Special Sales, Newmarket Press, 18 East 48th Street, New York, NY 10017; call (212) 832-3575 ext. 19 or 1-800-669-3903; FAX (212) 832-3629.

Manufactured in the United States of America

Special thanks to editor Linda Sunshine and designer Timothy Shaner at Night & Day Design (nightanddaydesign.biz).

Produced by Newmarket Press: Esther Margolis, President and Publisher; Frank DeMaio, Production Director; Keith Hollaman, Executive Editor; Paul Sugarman, Digital Supervisor

Other Newmarket Film and Entertainment Books include:

Angels and Demons: The Illustrated Movie Companion
Anonymous: William Shakespeare Revealed
The Art of How to Train Your Dragon
The Art of Monsters vs. Aliens
Bram Stoker's Dracula: The Film and the Legend*
Chicago: The Movie and Lyrics*
Dances with Wolves: The Illustrated Story of the Epic Film*
E.T. The Extra-Terrestrial: From Concept to Classic*
Gladiator: The Making of the Ridley Scott Epic Film
Good Night, and Good Luck: The Screenplay and History Behind the Landmark Movie*
Hotel Rwanda: Bringing the True Story of an African Hero to Film*
The Jaws Log
Making Tootsie: A Film Study with Dustin Hoffman & Sydney Pollack
Memoirs of a Geisha: A Portrait of the Film
Milk: A Pictorial History of Harvey Milk
The Mummy: Tomb of the Dragon Emperor
Ray: A Tribute to the Movie, the Music, and the Man*
Rescue Me: Uncensored
Saving Private Ryan: The Men, The Mission, The Movie
Schindler's List: Images of the Steven Spielberg Film
Titanic and the Making of James Cameron: The Inside Story of the Three-Year Adventure That Rewrote Motion Picture History

*Includes the screenplay

www.newmarketpress.com

RIGHT: Drawings by Peter de Sève, color by Evgeni Tomov.

Contents

PREFACE
by Peter Lord, *Producer,*
Co-founder of Aardman 7

FOREWORD
by Bob Osher, *President,*
Sony Pictures Digital Productions 9

INTRODUCTION
by Sarah Smith, *Director/Writer* 13

PART 1: The Beginnings
The Claus Family [Christmas] Tree . . 23
Arthur 30
Grandsanta 38
Santa 44
Mrs. Santa 47
Steve 50
Elves 56
Byrony 58
Peter 60

PART 2: "How Does He Do It?"
Beat Boards 72
Storyboards 74
Color Keys 76
Production Paintings 80
Arthur's Office 82
Old Sleigh Barn 90
Mission Control 98
The S-1 106

PART 3:
The World Outside the North Pole
Gwen 122
Toronto 128
Idaho 132
Africa 134
Mexico: The Wrong Trelew 140
Cayo de Confites, Cuba 142
Atlantic 144
UNFITA 146
Gwen Hines' Trelew,
    Including the 1,000-Yard Dash . . . 156

Acknowledgments 160

Preface

A Christmas Gift

How do you set about making an animated movie?

Well we've made a few here at Aardman, and the simple answer is: you start small—very small—with a tiny seed of an idea. Over years you nurture that idea, you shape it, build on it and allow it to evolve. Gradually the idea becomes visible through drawing, design, lighting and performance. It's always a heroic task and in the end it involves hundreds of people.

But as this is a Christmas film, and as I'm one of the producers, I hope you'll allow me a flight of fancy. I was thinking that *producing* a film is a little bit like opening the most amazing Christmas present you could dream of—but in extreme slow motion.

Imagine you were given a small, beautifully wrapped gift. That was me, five years ago, when Sarah Smith first told me the story that Pete Baynham had told *her*. It looks irresistible, it's so tantalizing! There's definitely something wonderful in here, but you can't quite guess what it is yet.

What can I tell you about that original idea that Sarah pitched to me so long ago? I can tell you that in detail the finished film is very different, and yet the big central ideas are intact. I can tell you that when I heard it I thought "now *there's* a movie!"—and I can tell you that such ideas come along very rarely in life.

So you take off the ribbon and start to unwrap it and—wouldn't you know—there's another wrapped gift inside, but it's slightly bigger than the first one—how is that possible? And of course when you unwrap that layer, there's another inside that one too, only maybe now it's a different shape, maybe now it seems to hint at a different sort of gift in the middle. You want to get to that lovely thing in the centre, which is the movie, but you can't hurry it and anyway, isn't the anticipation all part of the fun?

And so over five years, I've watched (and sometimes helped) this slow process of un-

LEFT: Alexei Nechytaylo and Stephen Hanson.

Preface

wrapping the gift. It's a beautiful and challenging process, and every layer is marked by surprise and delight and discovery.

Of course, while you and I can happily watch this process evolving, the filmmakers aren't really *unwrapping* a gift—they're making it, piece by tiny piece. Many brilliant artists and technicians exert all their efforts, really pushing themselves in a million ways. Sometimes the decisions they make are enormous and defining. Often they're so tiny that you'd never even think about it—how many lace-holes on an elf's boot? What texture is on the door handle on a closet in a child's room?

Well, that whole process is over now; the gift is revealed in all its glory. When you see how it's been made, you realize what a glorious collaboration it's been between the Aardman team in Bristol and the Sony team in Culver City. We've pooled the best of talents from both sides of the Atlantic to make a very British, but I believe universal film.

What incredible opportunities this film offers for design and artwork and characterization. We get to fly around the world from the Arctic, to the Serengeti and up into Space. We see the story-book beauty of Santa's sleigh flying across the Aurora Borealis, and we get to visit sleeping towns, cities and villages.

Sarah and her team have imagined the entire world of the Elves at the North Pole and created an enormous Control Centre carved out of ice. Now look at the graphic displays on all those computer consoles—every display is full of fun and charm—amazing little background jokes that you'll never notice when you first see the movie. And somebody's really worked out in detail how Santa's amazing mission is realized every year.

And of course, it's not just about the world. The story is totally rooted in character. It only works because Arthur and Grandsanta and Bryony really *live* through their design, vocal performance and animation.

So I'll leave you to immerse yourself in the creativity and the artistry, in the hard-work, inspiration and downright genius that has gone into the making of this beautiful film.

—PETER LORD
Producer, Co-founder of Aardman

Foreword

Imagination and Innovation

There's nothing more fun than watching those two progressive forces of ingenuity work together, pushing each other to greater things.

That's the foundation of the relationship between the creative crew at Aardman Animations and the inventive team at Sony Pictures Digital Productions, two enterprising entities that have now forged a bond for present and future films—starting with *Arthur Christmas*.

As a longtime fan of Aardman's moviemaking style, I was thrilled to see this marriage come together. In many ways, *Arthur Christmas* represents the merging of two distinct filmmaking approaches: Aardman's classic stop-frame movies such as *Chicken Run* and the Wallace and Gromit stories, and Sony's groundbreaking CG techniques employed in films like *Cloudy with a Chance of Meatballs*, *Surf's Up* and, most recently, *The Smurfs*.

The shared creative vision for this relationship was simple: Sony Pictures Digital Productions' creative, technological, financial, distribution and marketing resources would enable Aardman to make movies in their unique style, and allow their original characters and stories to grace the largest possible stage for all the world to see.

Arthur Christmas fits perfectly into the untethered philosophy of Sony Pictures Animation, a division of Sony Pictures Digital Productions, where each film stands on its own unique and original style and design. Simultaneously, our visual effects division—Sony Pictures Imageworks—continues to enhance its reputation and expand its proficiency with landmark work on such films as *Alice in Wonderland*. Regardless of the look of any given film, the "story" is always first and foremost our main concern.

Sony Pictures Digital Productions' unparalleled diversity of projects allows us to both understand a wide expanse of design cues and influences, and learn and grow with each project we undertake. The end result is an optimum expansion of our expertise that ultimately benefits every future project.

Foreword

At this moment, *Arthur Christmas* is reaping the huge rewards of that experience and, at the same time, Aardman's collective imagination is pushing our innovative envelope to new horizons. From the start, no one sought to make *Arthur Christmas* into a CG film that looked like a traditional Aardman stop-frame animated film. As revered as their patented stop-frame techniques are, the true gold in Aardman's animation style is their incredible attention to detail and loving sense of handcraftsmanship. Taking Aardman to a CG format has only encouraged those strengths, paving the way for detail that couldn't be replicated otherwise.

Arthur Christmas is a film to be savored in every frame of its incredible detail. From hilarious sight gags to subtle design elements, there isn't a moment the screen doesn't glow with visual reminders of the animators' touch. Look closely and you'll see exactly what I mean, whether it be in the varied identifiable-by-badge ranks of the elves, the hundreds of holiday-themed knick-knacks displayed in Arthur's office, or the subtle Christmas tree tread-marks of Steve's shoes in freshly fallen snow. It's all there, right down to the tactile Aardman touch in the film's color and lighting keys, made possible through a combination of the Aardman aesthetic with advanced technologies developed at Sony Pictures Imageworks.

While no detail has been spared, *Arthur Christmas* also boasts an unprecedented sense of scale and space. Millions of elves scurry about Mission Control at the North Pole, and more than 15,000 of the fastidious little fellows are present on the S-1—a state-of-the-art sleigh the size of a small city. When this film isn't astounding audiences with the magnitude of a grand scale aerial assault in the delivery of gifts on Christmas Eve, it's gallivanting from Denmark to Africa to Idaho and Toronto—offering wonderful visual representations of the distinct cultures of each realm during Arthur's heart-warming quest to ensure no child is forgotten on Christmas morning.

The film's international flavor extends far beyond the screen. We've been in development on this film since the summer of 2007 when the effusive Pete Baynham and indefatigable Sarah Smith pitched the idea to Sony. We loved the concept from the very first. In Bristol, UK, the Aardman team, with input from Sony, developed the script and came up with visual concepts and ideas. Moving back and forth between Bristol and Los Angeles has been part of the process ever since. A group of Aardman creatives moved to California for a few years, and several Sony personnel shifted residences to England for a year or more during pre-production. Hannah Minghella (former President of Production for Sony Pictures Animation) and I would visit Bristol every other month, and Peter Lord and David Sproxton (co-founders of Aardman and producers of *Arthur Christmas*) also frequently made trips to Culver City. They were very involved in all aspects of this movie, and their creativity and insights have been extraordinary.

Distance and time differences aside, the partnership has been exemplary. It's been a nice melding of cultures; we've taught and learned a great deal from each other. The results are obvious—*Arthur Christmas* will be that calling card. Moreover, we're already hard at work on our next collaboration: *The Pirates! Band of Misfits*, a stop-frame feature directed by Peter Lord and coming to theatres in early 2012.

This is the beginning of a beautiful friendship. How beautiful? Turn the pages and see for yourself.

—BOB OSHER
President, Sony Pictures Digital Productions

DEAR SANTA

MY FREIND DOSN'T **BELIEVE** IN YOU CAUSE TO GET ROUND ALL THE CHILDREN IN THE WORLD IN ONE NIGHT YOU'D HAVE TO GO SO FAST IT WOULD MAKE YOU AND THE SLEIGH AND THE REINDEER BURN UP... I THINK YOU ARE REAL BUT HOW DO YOU DO IT? FOR CHRISTMAS I WOULD LOVE A PINK TWINKLE BICYCLE WITH STABELISERS BUT PLEASE! DONT BRING IT IF IT MAKES THE RIENDEER BURN.

LOVE GWEN HINES
23 MIMOSA AVENUE
TRELEW CORNWALL
ENGLAND

Introduction

It Could Be True . . .

On this page you will find the three pieces of development artwork that all animated movies produce, in which we nailed the look of our movie.

Or rather, this is where you would find them *if* we'd ever managed to come up with them. . . .

In fact, our walls were terrifyingly bare of the kind of pictures people point at when executives visit and ask the (literally) multimillion-dollar question, "So, what will it *look* like?"

The first trailer we made for *Arthur Christmas* featured an anxious elf trying to divert the attention of a camera crew from Santa's secret North Pole by pointing limply in the other direction and exclaiming desperately, "Polar bear! In a hat!"

For many months, this was the modus operandi of the *Arthur Christmas* team. What it will look like? Um . . . here, look at these amazing textures! See this great reference for Gwen's house! How about the pattern on Steve's suit?! Er . . . polar bear! In a hat!

That is of course when we HAD a team. For the first eighteen months I was developing the "team" there was myself and my assistant, Alice. Not only did we have no concept art, we had no story artists, no designer, no art team and no pipeline in which to produce a CG movie even if we *could* work out what it should look like. And since Aardman had not at that point signed with Sony, we had no budget or distributor.

All we had was the benign creative nest that is Aardman; me, Pete Baynham . . . and a big idea.

Pete Baynham was one of the first people I called when I joined Aardman. The timing was propitious. "I think I may just have come up with one of the best ideas I've ever had," he told me. He pitched me in three minutes the basis of *Arthur Christmas*—and I agreed. You just KNOW when you hear an idea like that, an idea that you can't believe no one has thought of before, because it feels so natural and classic. Christmas as a huge military operation, one child missed . . .

We started work on the storyline together; the movie we have now is the child of our long, hilariously argumentative and deeply fond friendship. Twenty years of shared jokes found their way into the film. We love comedy, but we also both love big emotional stories

OPPOSITE: Alexei Nechytaylo and Sam Davis.

Introduction

and passionately believe that you have to put some part of your own truth into a story. If you're not prepared to put on the line something that you feel very personally and vulnerably, then I believe no one else will feel anything when they watch it. Whenever we were reaching for emotional moments we would keep pitching lines and ideas at each other till one of us touched the other to the point of tears. Then it went on paper.

And as well as emotionally truthful, we wanted the whole story to be shot through with a feeling of authenticity: "It *could* be true!" We wanted to respect all the beliefs children have about Santa and to add to these, to extend their faith. Environments, process, technology, scale, detail, everything should feel credible so that viewers watching the film would have a sense of recognition—"Of *course!* That's how Santa does it! That's how he lives these days." We worked on every bit of logic, every aspect of the world we were creating to give it complete integrity.

So what did that mean for design? For me, coming from live action, CG design was a bit of a shock. Not only did every location have to be imagined rather than scouted, I am used to my actors turning up on set with their own noses. Now someone was asking me to make decisions on the depth and color of a nostril!

The world of CG design is so infinitely open and flexible, it is both fabulous and bemusing. I rapidly understood the calming comfort of being able to pick up some book of paintings featuring the charmingly stylized work of some artist or other and declaring authoritatively, "It will look like this!" We never found such a simple, defining influence. To me, style should match content. And our content was about the real, natural, contemporary world that every child knows.

Back we came to our guiding idea: "It could be true . . ." The world of the film should feel like the world as a child imagines it outside their bedroom window on Christmas night: They know it's still the same streets and garages and towns out there, but somehow everything feels glittering and heightened in the sparkling magic of Christmas night.

We decided to chase a storybook look based on a very "real" world. Locations would feel real but heightened in layout or lighting—as though we just happened to have found the most perfect street, gas station, shop, cul-de-sac in the "real" world, Tim Burton style. From Roger Deakins, we saw landscapes transformed into paintings in *No Country for Old Men,* and worked on composition to organize a naturalistic world into storybook images.

And striding, leaping, cycling through these environments were our characters. Of course they had to be stylized for animation, but did stylized really mean that they had to end up looking like toys from a mold, perfect, symmetrical, polished, plasticized? Aardman's stop-frame characters have a particular quirky, imperfect charm, qualities that come naturally with plasticine. They have never sought per se to look appealing and cute—they *are* charming because of the personalities they represent. We did not want the characters to look in any way like stop-frame puppets; but we wanted them to come from the same family as Aardman's characters. We wanted them to feel particular and British.

And so, leaning on the artistry of Evgeni Tomov, the brilliance of art directors Alexei Nechytaylo and Olivier Adam, and the creative partnership of Doug Ikeler from Sony Imageworks, and all those who followed them, we stumbled forwards, with as many nos as yeses. Evgeni's painting of Arthur in Trelew (see page 156)—a little too romantic, colored and heightened; Steve Hanson's portrait of Gwen's bedroom (page 122)—too cute and chunky, too *Monsters, Inc.*, too "animation!"; Hanson's image of Aarhus (pages 70-71)—too live action. But nobody worry, we have beautiful story-reels coming along! Polar bear, in a hat!

Yet step by step, the team found its way to discovering a look that is so much more than the sum of its parts.

And when I finally saw the very first shots that were rendered, of Arthur and Grandsanta talking in the Old Sleigh Barn, I was absolutely totally gob-smacked. It was so amazing and gorgeous and different and unexpected and unlike anything I'd ever seen, I was in a turmoil of emotion, from elation to terror.

And it was then I knew. THAT'S what the movie looks like!
—SARAH SMITH, *Director/Writer*

OPPOSITE: Alexei Nechytaylo and Sam Davis.

NORTH POLE

Dear Gwen

Thank you for your letter and <u>brilliant</u> picture. Your request for a pink twinkle bike will be passed to Santa. <u>YES, DO BELIEVE</u> in Santa, he is <u>REAL!</u> And he CAN get around the world to EVERY child without a single reindeer being ~~hurt~~ hurt. By the time the sun comes up on Christmas day he'll get to <u>you too!</u> Using his special

MAGIC

MAIL AGENT 3776

Christmas Comes Early to Sony and Aardman

I grew up in England with some of the very early Aardman characters, even before *Wallace and Gromit*. As an English person, Aardman is imprinted in your mind as being part of our entertainment culture. It's incredibly British. What is wonderful about Aardman is that they are completely uncompromising in their art, in the way of only the most talented and creative people. They have a real specificity in their style of comedy and their look.

In the late fall of 2007, shortly after Aardman and Dreamworks announced their separation and even before I started working at Sony Animation, I went with Amy Pascal, Michael Lynton and Bob Osher to the UK to talk with Aardman about bringing their studio into a partnership with Sony.

At that first meeting, Aardman presented a number of projects that were in very early development. These were ideas they had or were hoping to work on in the future and *Arthur Christmas* was one of them. Even though they had not yet started to work on it, the idea was very fully formed for Sarah Smith and Pete Baynham. They had really funny, detailed ideas for moments and characters that felt incredibly fresh and original. The story married traditional values with contemporary ideas and, from the very specific to the larger themes they wanted to explore, the idea felt like it could work on many levels. We immediately loved it. We all thought it was very much in the spirit of what animation can do best and how it can bring worlds and characters to life.

We talked about how we could capture the essence of Aardman in a CG film so that they wouldn't get lost. I think that was accomplished with the attention to detail and having the comedy come from characters who are a little bit eccentric and certainly British in their eccentricity.

Arthur Christmas plays on a bigger world stage perhaps than any previous Aardman movie but their primary characters and their personalities are still quintessentially British and have an Aardman edge. In some of the character designs they were able to capture that Aardman look even though you don't quite get the feel of the stop-motion movies.

It's interesting to recall that first meeting today because the spirit of the film Sarah Smith pitched back then—the one she had in mind to make—is very much the movie they ultimately created.

—Hannah Minghella, President of Production, Columbia Pictures; former Head of Production, Sony Pictures Animation

Freely Plundered

There's a stage when your film is so tiny, it's a single cell creature that can turn into anything from an eel to a mastodon. Everything is up for grabs. Everything is possible. So we probably did discuss the idea of making this as a stop-frame but we were ambitious to make a CG film. From a practical point of view, to be honest, we can only make one stop-frame film at a time. So it didn't take very long to identify *Arthur Christmas* as particularly well designed for CG with its vast cast and lots of flying around the world.

Making a CG film is a mammoth undertaking and I'm interested in the philosophy and spirit of how a studio works. There was no pressure to work with Sony. We considered working all over the world and talked to people in London, Paris, and even Sydney. We explored all the options.

When we looked at the tools Sony offered, the experience and of course the people, it was obvious we should work with them. Sony also comes with a great philosophy and spirit, as well as talent and technology. In the early days we were interested in people like Doug Ikeler, a fantastic can-do kind of fellow who was totally supportive of our vision. He got what we were trying to do, what Sarah wanted to do, the Aardman feel and how we work as a studio. Sony was an incredible resource for designers, story people, storyboarders, lighters, texturers, and riggers. We've plundered freely from them.

—Peter Lord, producer, Co-founder of Aardman

A Long, Long Journey to Take

Arthur Christmas is a hugely ambitious project, especially for Sarah Smith who is a first-time director. We supported her from the very first but warned her the workload would be massive. There are so many departments and so much going through the pipeline that a CG or stop-motion movie is a five-year haul, which is a long, long journey to take. The interesting thing is that about three and a half of those years are about script development, writing, design work and character development. The actual production takes about eighteen months.

—David Sproxton, producer, Co-founder of Aardman

Yes, It's Going to Hurt

Live action is my background and I brought that sensibility to CG. So if a character falls over he is not going to bounce; it is going to hurt. I wanted to make all the characters feel truthful and not replace what a child believes. I think animation makes it possible to believe in a way that live action could not.

I care a lot about the look of the film, which is incredibly unique and doesn't look like any other CG film. The movie was entirely eclectic and the style was particular to whatever scene we were designing. We never had one simple design style that would fit every scene in the movie and define how the movie would look throughout. Though each scene is different, the overall feel is that the textures and the detailing are almost photorealistic and look like photography. The art is full of realistic details but presented in a kind of idealized way.

—Sarah Smith, director/writer

Immense Talent and Effort

Aardman philosophy has always been to create working environments where directors can thrive, and empower the crew to do their best work.

Arthur Christmas is an original idea by Pete Baynham (Borat and Bruno), brought to studio and developed by Sarah Smith; they share writing credit with Sarah directing. The two have worked together for many years and have an exciting creative bond. One big disadvantage when we started was that Pete lived in Los Angeles. We managed to turn this around when we discovered that he and Sarah had a fascinating working relationship. Sarah worked at Aardman in Bristol during the day and when she went home at night, when everyone else was going to sleep, she would start working with Pete via Skype. So when we moved everyone to LA it was fantastic to put Sarah and Pete together in one place, although we did discover that, what with LA traffic, we wound up using Skype almost as much here as we did in the UK.

Each film requires something slightly different; this film had a slight logistical challenge called the "Atlantic." Logistical challenges included moving the team mid-production, setting up a seamless process of digital communication, keeping an animation team going in Bristol (which was really important to Aardman), learning to drive on the wrong side of the road and buying enough English tea.

—Steve Pegram, producer

Relocation

Arthur Christmas is such a big, ambitious film that we probably underestimated how long it would take, particularly in terms of design. Previously our directors have had a strong hand in the design process. Nick Park will often do many of the early drawings himself. This process was quite different. We had to create so many different locations all requiring very different design styles. We did an awful lot of early concept design and sourced artists from all over the world—France, US, UK, Canada, Spain, and Germany.

Relocating people around the world was quite a challenge. This was a team of people who had never worked together before, having to move to countries they had never lived in before, working with a director who had never directed an animated movie before! . . . We managed to assemble a truly international and amazingly talented group of people and I think it's partly this diversity that has led us to achieving a very unique look to the film.

—Carla Shelley, producer

Between England and LA

From a producing point of view, having the teams separated between England and LA was the biggest challenge. Filmmaking is an intimate process and doing it from afar is complicated. The logistics of making decisions was much harder between the different time zones. From a technology standpoint, the scope of the movie was also a challenge. It's a large-scale movie so the amount of work, plus the fact that it is a traveling film with numerous locations made it complicated.

—Chris Juen, Co-producer

A British Element

There's certainly a British sensibility to our work in the way we tell our stories and our use of British voices in casting our films. However, we think that a good story should have universal appeal. A story about cricket probably wouldn't play in America, though it would do incredibly well in India. There are areas where we're careful to make sure the language, in terms of the nuances and colloquialisms, will translate to an American audience.

I don't know how true this is but it's often said that the British have a great sense of irony. Our TV comedy, for example, is based on characters that are losers at the bottom of the food chain, like David in "The Office." American comedy tends to be slightly more aspirational, like "Cheers," "Friends" or "Sex in the City." That's a fundamental difference.

This is our first movie with Sony and our working relationships with Hannah, Bob, Amy and Michael has been very good. We put together a key creative team in the UK and then went to the US to drive the pipeline.

We learn something new with every film. *Arthur Christmas* is an emotional movie with more heart than our past films. It's played less for gags, though it has a lot of comedy. Sony has been hugely supportive with great editorial input and an amazing team.

—David Sproxton, producer, Co-founder of Aardman

EARLY ART AND STORY

The very earliest art for *Arthur Christmas* was the product of a three-month trip to Venice, California. We set up shop in a photographer's studio, with three computers and some models of Wallace and Gromit. Pete and I wrote the first draft of the script in the garden, and at the same time launched some exploratory artwork, in an attempt to find an art and story team.

It was a bit like being part of a Victorian expedition; we arrived from the other side of the world quaintly over-dressed with a large quantity of boxes and the name of a local guide on the back of an envelope, with an unformed plan to map the unknown jungle of CG filmmaking. A procession of talent left us with some fascinating imagery, including illustrations by Buck Lewis, George Hull and Armand Serrano.

Working remotely in Germany, independent short filmmaker Till Nowak designed, modeled, textured and lit an extraordinarily detailed and visionary first 3D version of Mission Control, the S-1 dock, the North Pole and the Arctic. He animated the S-1 to fly home to the pole, underwater and into the dock, and animated cameras to give sweeping shots of the environment. He achieved the whole thing, entirely alone, in *three weeks*. It's an incredible feat. He provided visual ideas that made it into final movie.

In the end, the design team came not from the Venice trip, but closer to home. Returning to England we visited the production of the very beautiful *Tales of Despereaux* in London, and hired the European art team, designer Evgeni Tomov and art directors Olivier Adam and Alexei Nechytaylo.

—Sarah Smith, director/writer

TOP LEFT: Armand Serrano. TOP RIGHT: Till Nowak. LEFT: George Hull. ABOVE RIGHT: Buck Lewis.

The Santa Family (Christmas) Tree

Aliens or Elves?

About six years ago I had this thought: How does Santa do it? I mean, literally, how does he do all that in one night? The idea of the sleigh and reindeer just seemed too improbable. So I thought maybe he has a kind of ship, like the one in *Independence Day*. I remember looking at a poster of that movie and wondering, what if that wasn't bad aliens bent on our destruction in the ship? What if it was Santa and millions of elves?

At the same time, I started wondering what would happen if Santa got ill and his idiot son had to deliver the presents. Did Santa have a father or children? How is Santa even around if he started in the 4th century? There must be a lineage of Santas. That means that maybe Santa has a son waiting in the wings to take over, like Prince Charles waiting for the Queen to abdicate. That seemed like another comic idea for a movie. Then I combined both of those ideas.

When I got this idea of this lineage of Santas, I began to wonder what Grandsanta would be like. Would he be like my grandmother? It seemed like a funny idea to have Grandsanta being against the modern ways and stuck in the past.

Marrying all the massive technology involved in delivering presents around the world with the magic of Christmas is what really interested me. As a kid, I was totally into the magic of Christmas. The fun of it came with mixing all the seriousness of Mission Control with the mission of getting a present to one particular kid. This giant operation is all about keeping kids in that magical belief that Santa is arriving in a sleigh.

—Pete Baynham, screenwriter

OPPOSITE: Michael Kurinsky.
BELOW: Alexei Nechytaylo, Jerry Loveland, Stephen Hanson, Tim Watts.

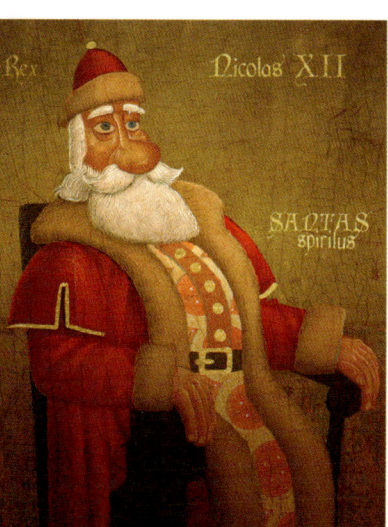

Making It Real

The film has quite a realistic feeling, as Sarah's main objective was to create a believable movie. She didn't want an artificial, totally designed or created world. She wanted the film to resonate with the audience in a palpable way. Of course, the characters are a bit more stylized, but the environment and feeling of the world is quite authentic.

—Evgeni Tomov, production designer

Funny But Flawed

At Aardman, we believe in stories based on character. Our instinct is to find strong, flawed characters that we like. We look for characters who are less than perfect because they make for the best drama and the most comedy. We try to find the comedic heart to any story. *Arthur Christmas* is not a hugely broad comedy but what tickled us was this family of quirky characters, each with a different take on Christmas. That seemed like a place where we would have fun.

—Peter Lord, producer, Co-founder of Aardman

TOP (left and right): Barry Raynolds, Jerry Loveland, Michael Kurinsky, Stephen Hanson, Tim Watts.
MIDDLE and BELOW: Tim Watts.
OPPOSITE: Tim Watts and Michael Kurinsky.

ABOVE: Evgeni Tomov, the first design of Santa.
RIGHT: Tim Watts, Michael Kurinsky, Evgeni Tomov.

Characters

I was desperate not to reproduce the CG humans I had seen elsewhere, that felt somehow mass-made. So Pete de Sève did not set about designing characters per se. I described to him who they *were,* and he drew them not as pleasing outlines but as personalities. Then we pored over the multiple images and honed in on what were to become the design principles for each character.

As the characters took shape we brought in live-action costume designer Yves Barre, much awarded for the work we did together on BBC Television's *The League of Gentlemen.* He arrived with twin sets for Mrs. Santa with holly patterns embroidered at the neck, designs for elf camouflage, Goretex and fur samples for Santa and an armful of hideous Christmas jumpers, to add another layer of verité detail to the world.

—Sarah Smith, director/writer

A Question of Style

The immediate question when we first met with Aardman was to ask if they wanted a stop-motion look to this film. Both Peter Lord and Sarah Smith were emphatic that that was not what they wanted. That was a great relief to me because although stop motion has great benefits when you are in that world I don't think it makes sense to imitate it in CG.

We tried to emulate classic Aardman style, especially in the characters. There's a tactile nature to stop motion that, when you see it, it makes you want to touch it. Anything that is too smooth or too perfect looking does not belong in a stop-motion world so we tried to highjack that aspect of their style.

—Doug Ikeler, VFX supervisor

Look to the Nose

We wanted the characters to be a little more anatomical and subtle in terms of the modeling whilst retaining the simple kinds of shapes typical of other Aardman designs. We also tried to find a resemblance between the different members of the Santa family. In terms of unifying them, we looked at their noses. In profile they all have this sort of ski jump nose. Arthur has the longest, slimmest nose, progressing through the others to Grandsanta, whose nose is more squat and bulbous. You can also see a similarity in the distance between the eyes and the shape of the face.

—Tim Watts, character design art director

Favorite Moments

One of my favorite moments working on this project happened the first day we showed final lit shots for director approval. After years of development and lots of reviews looking at grey characters the moment had come to see it come to life. Instead of watching the shot on the screen, I was looking at Sarah to see her reaction—and it was one of pure joy, like someone who had just been given the best Christmas gift. Another moment like this came very close to the end of the production schedule, when Pete Baynham came in to see how things were going, and he literally gasped and then jumped on the sofa in excitement. These were fabulous moments that left the entire team walking a little straighter when they came out of the review.

—Mandy Tankenson, digital producer

Quirky Sense of Quiet

The Aardman sensibility is grounded in a quirkier sense of a quieter character. The characters aren't overacting or being overly broad but there's a sincerity to them that makes them very appealing in a familiar way. You can always compare their characters to people you know, to people who've been in your life and that kind of quick accessibility makes their stories so strong.

Aardman isn't about constant flash or explosions. You can stay with their characters on their journey through the movie and that makes you root for them. Putting the character first is the mandate for all animated films but Aardman does it particularly well.

—Donnie Long, head of story

ABOVE: Early concept drawing by Peter de Sève.

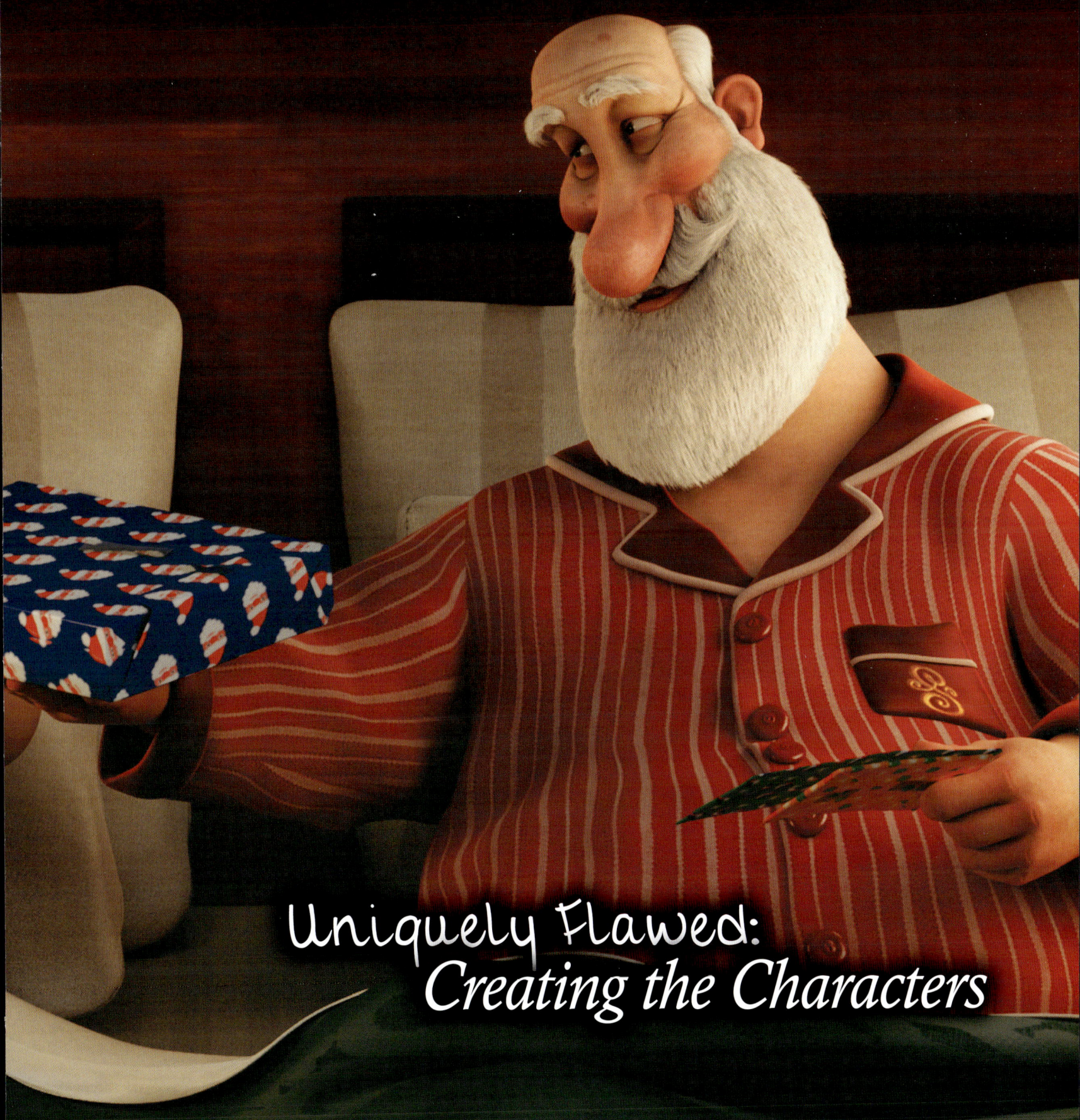

Uniquely Flawed:
Creating the Characters

Arthur believes in Christmas and not just because he's been born into the family business. He believes it in his soul— there's nobody in the world who cares about Christmas more than Arthur.
—James McAvoy

I have to worry. It's the only thing I'm good at.
—Arthur

Arthur
voiced by James McAvoy

Despite living in a world devoted year-round to the business of Christmas, Arthur LOVES everything to do with the season. He is especially passionate about what Santa—who he adores as both dad and figurehead—means to children, whose identities sometimes get lost in the huge logistics of the operation. Trouble is, in the ultra-efficient, high-tech delivery operation of Christmas, Santa's youngest son is a spare part. Allergic to snow and suffering from a fear of heights, reindeer, and high-speed travel, Arthur isn't exactly a natural Claus. The family loves him—but has never quite known what to do with him. But although Arthur's office in the Letters Department is a chaotic mess of snow globes and pictures of Santa, it's a magical little corner where Arthur alone revels in the joy of it all. In Santa he believes.

Skinny Bloke

Arthur is energetic, nerdy, a bit weedy. A skinny bloke. That's who he is. At one point Pete de Sève tried drawing him plump, against expectation. No one believed in it. But everyone had seen long skinny under-dogs in animation before. In Pete de Sève's drawings, it was clear clothes could give him his unique shape—his huge beloved Christmas jumpers, his big soft furry reindeer slippers. With skinny legs in between he had an original silhouette.

—Sarah Smith, director/writer

ABOVE: *Peter de Sève.*
RIGHT: *Early concept drawing for Arthur by Zébé.*

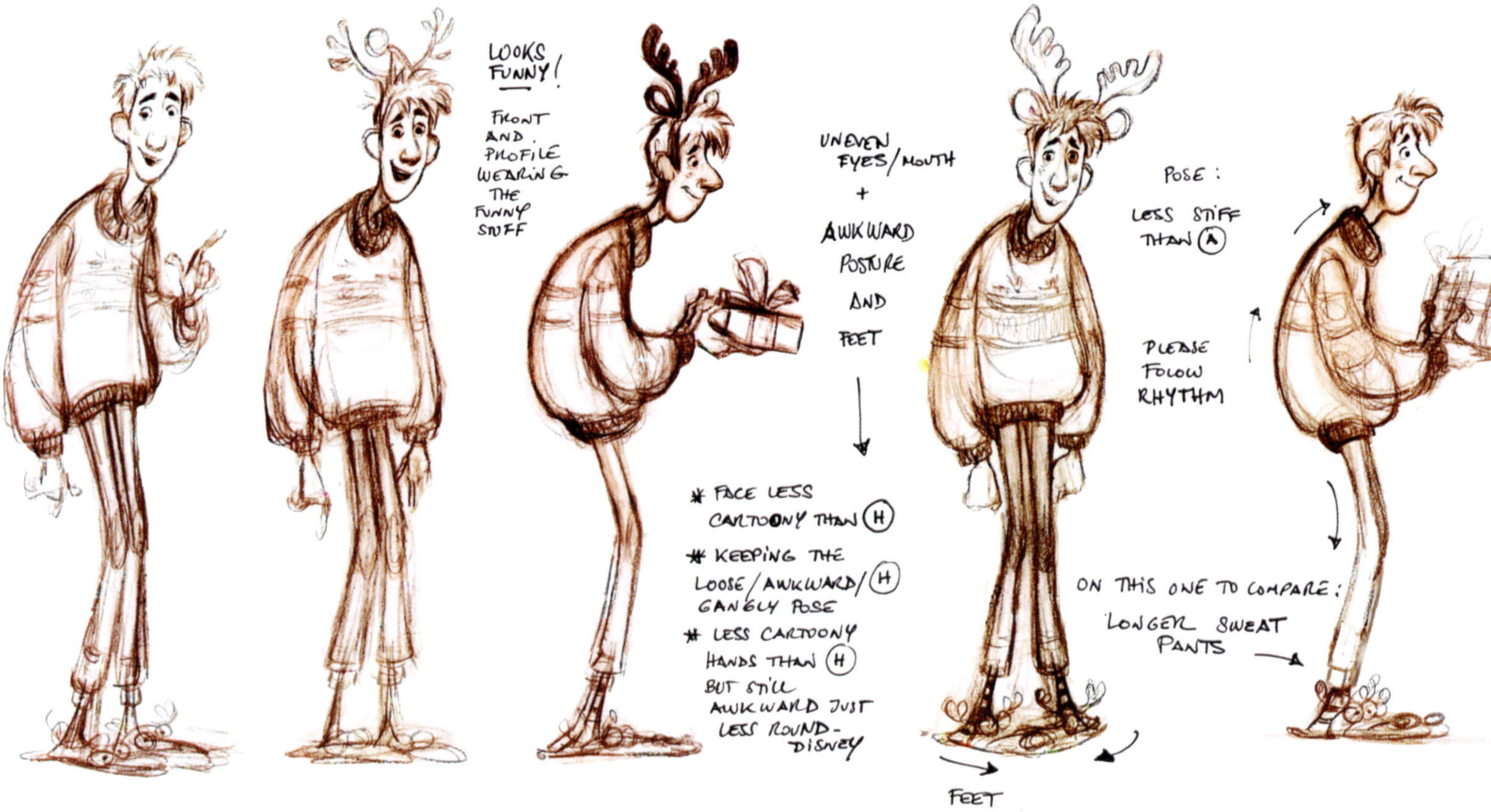

A Mess of Phobias

Arthur is a mess of phobias. He's allergic to snow. He's afraid of heights. He has a phobia about being beheaded. He's afraid of buttons.

—Pete Baynham, screenwriter

A Gentle Giant

Finding the hero in a story is always the most difficult part of character design in my experience. He/she has to be appealing in a general way but also unique. I cast a pretty wide net in my sketches until finally hitting upon the Arthur that appears in the film. He's a gentle giant, which is why I drew him stooping the way very tall people sometimes do unconsciously so they don't stand out. As a side note, more than one person has said that Arthur looks like me, but on steroids. It wouldn't be the first time this has happened. In fact, I think character designers often draw themselves without knowing it. It's an occupational hazard.

—Peter de Sève, concept character designer

Are You Arthur?

I think Arthur must be based on Pete [Baynham, the screenwriter], he was in the edit suite a couple of weeks ago when he managed to tip over a table, upending his laptop which crashed to the floor, then knocked over his coffee all in a single move. It's always amusing when Pete is around.

—James Cooper, editor

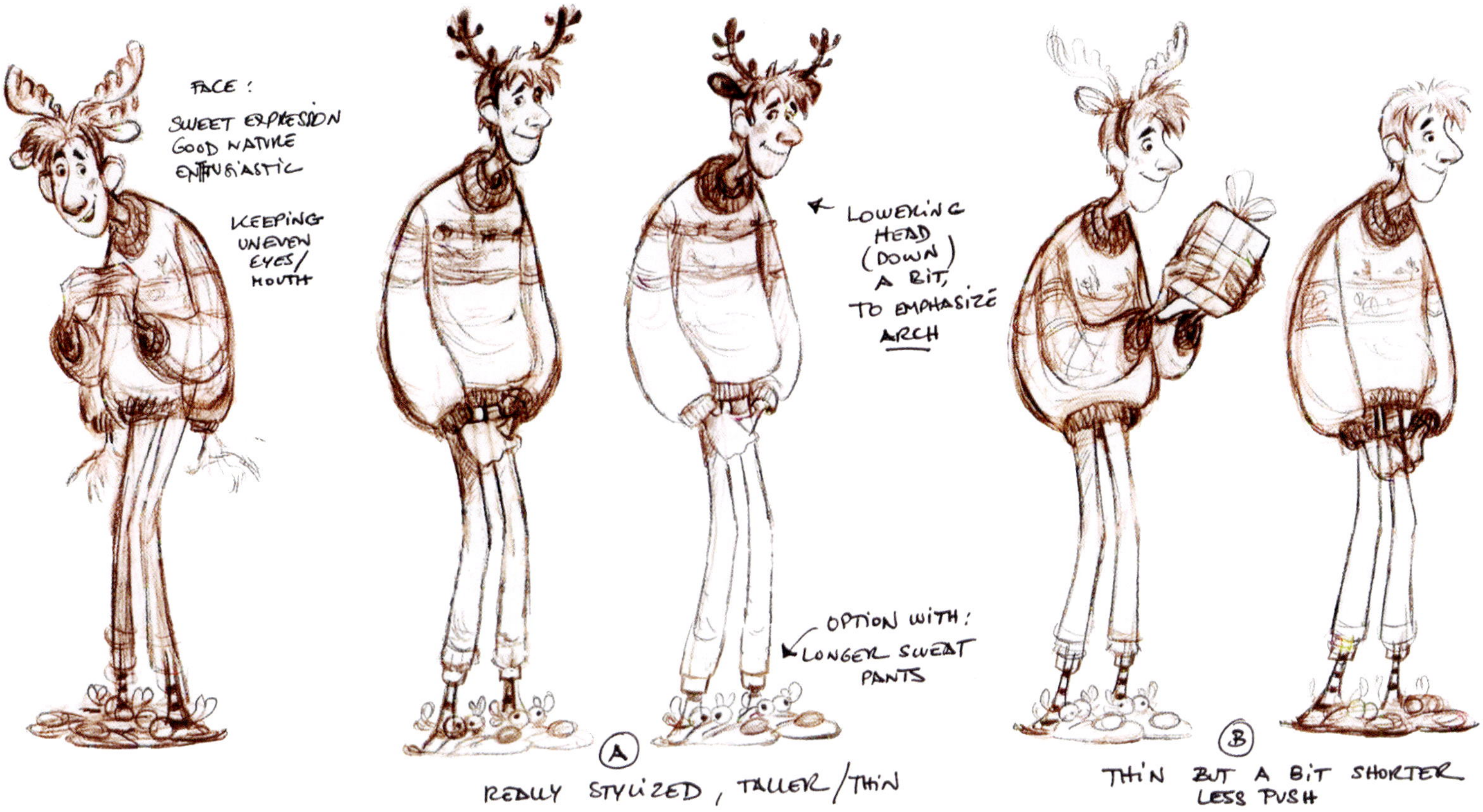

ABOVE: Carlos Grangel.
LEFT: Peter de Sève.
OPPOSITE: Tim Watts.

Arthur C'est Moi

I am lucky I've got a career as a writer because I really can't do anything else. I used to be in the merchant navy, which was a ridiculous decision for me because I am like Arthur. They would send me to get something and I'd be found 4 hours later. I'm staring off into space most of the time. I have no common sense. Also, I'm super into the whole magic of it all in a childlike way.

—Pete Baynham, screenwriter

A Nice Notion

People tend to pull stories from their own experience. When you talk to Pete about his upbringing, he'll say he was the runt of his Welsh family. He couldn't play rugby so he had to make his mark in comedy. Is he the prototype for Arthur? I never thought of him in those terms and I don't think he is quite such a clumsy or uncoordinated character—but it's a nice notion.

—David Sproxton, producer, Co-founder of Aardman

The Face of Arthur

At first we had a slightly more complicated shape to Arthur's face, actually more in line with the other character's faces; it was sort of like a peanut from the front. We showed this to Sarah and she said she needed to think. Next day she came back and said she thought that a simpler shape was required, something that would be clear and recognizable for him. In the end he wound up with a U- or soft V-shaped face. I think it worked out for the best because it is more immediate and easier to latch onto. Hopefully, that will be more memorable.

—TIM WATTS, CHARACTER DESIGN ART DIRECTOR

The Americanization of Arthur

Arthur Christmas has not been Americanized by the work that was done in Los Angeles but it has been influenced by some of Sarah's references within the lexicon of films that Hollywood had traditionally made. It was important to her to have the scale and scope of those films without compromising that very Aardman or British sensibility. She achieved that.

—HANNAH MINGHELLA, PRESIDENT OF PRODUCTION, COLUMBIA PICTURES; FORMER HEAD OF PRODUCTION, SONY PICTURES ANIMATION.

ABOVE: Tim Watts.
RIGHT: Arthur face painting by Evgeni Tomov.

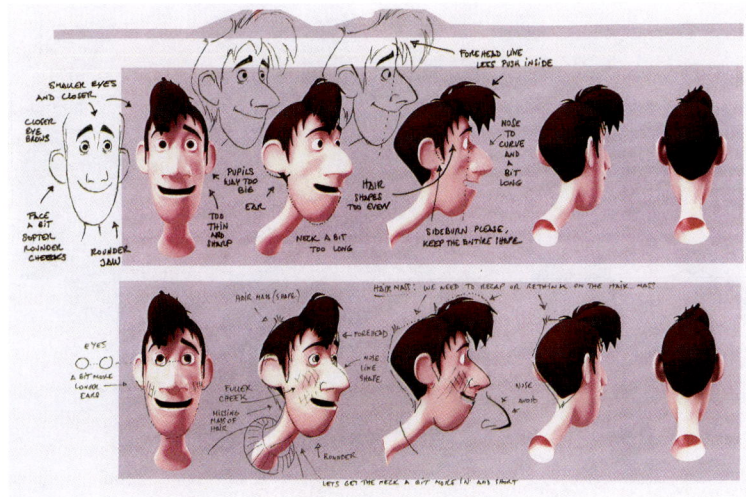

ABOVE and LEFT: Very early sketches and CG models by Carlos Grangel.

A Hands-On Stake

From the start *Arthur Christmas* always felt like a British film. The characters are very much in keeping with Aardman in that there is nothing perfect about them. Arthur even has some pimples on his chin. They feel very original, and there is something totally authentic and genuine about them all. The film also has a distinctive, tactile look to it—the detailing and textures make it feel very "handmade". . . quite unusual for a CG film. Again, this feels very true to Aardman's style.

—Carla Shelley, producer

Oh Those Slippers!

The characters didn't try to be cute or appealing. We tried to make them look more broken up. Arthur was the biggest challenge. The designers gave him a big wooly jumper and once I saw those gorgeous furry slippers I said he had to wear them throughout the movie.

—Sarah Smith, director/writer

Live-Action Mentality

Sarah Smith, the director, brought a live-action mentality to the CG world. She approaches everything from a live-action perspective. She hired a real costume designer to get the look and feel of different textures and clothes.

—Chris Juen, co-producer

LEFT: Slippers by Alexei Nechytaylo.
BELOW: Early ideas for Arthur's sweater by Zébé.

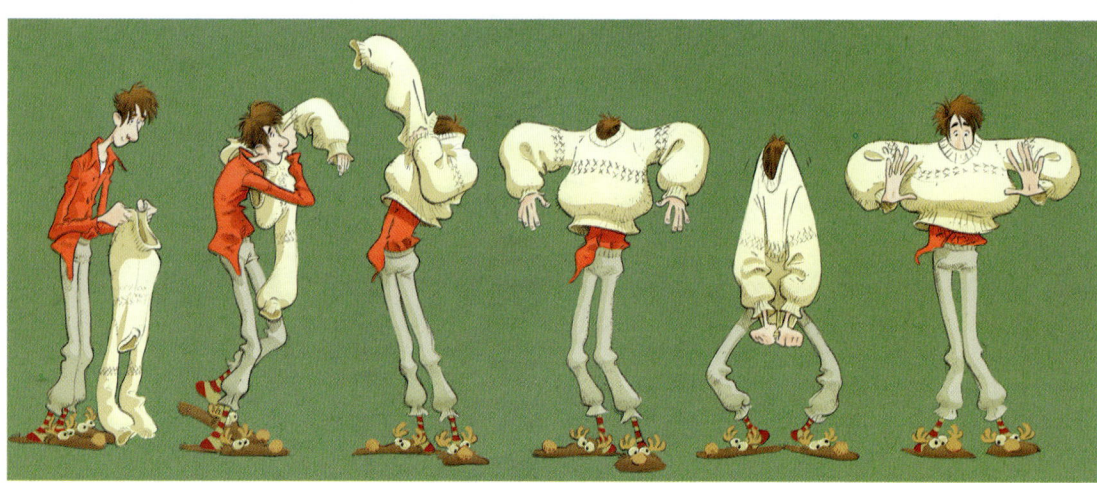

ARTHUR'S SWEATER

The thing about Arthur is that he is a skinny guy and his sweater does not fit him. It's the big wool sweater everyone has, but nobody wants. It's not comfortable but it says winter and it screams Christmas. The problem is making the sweater move when Arthur moves. All of our simulations are reality-based so it had to look real. But we didn't have a big enough body underneath the sweater to fill it out. We wanted to maintain a bell shape around Arthur's body but it was a battle not to have too many folds and bulk that would overwhelm the character. We couldn't let the sweater just hang. We had a menagerie of cheats to get that sweater looking right.
—Doug Ikeler, VFX supervisor

ABOVE LEFT: *Drawings of the sweater by Yves Barre.*
ABOVE RIGHT: *Alexei Nechytaylo.*
BELOW: *Aardman's Philip Child was the inspiration for the look of Arthur's hair. Here he wears 3 sweaters to help the artists recreate the look of bulky wool.*

In the real world on a real actor, a sweater can only be so special but our animated sweater—which has all this fur embedded in it—is luminous, outrageous, horrible but somehow gorgeous.
—Pete Baynham, screenwriter

In my day I didn't need a trillion elves in bleepy hats!
—Grandsanta

Grandsanta

voiced by Bill Nighy

The previous Santa Claus, now 136, is the archetypal old codger who complains constantly that "things were better in my day," when he used to go out in a lovely red sleigh pulled by eight beautiful reindeer. A hilariously politically incorrect old man who always speaks his mind, frail old Grandsanta may have been put out to pasture, but he's still a proud man who has never fully adjusted to retirement. Arthur's mission just might be the thing to pull him back in for one more go.

And if a child wakes up during his mission, he has the perfect solution: "A whack on the head with a sock-full of sand and a dab of whisky on the lips, they don't remember in the morning!"

ABOVE: Evgeni Tomov.
BELOW: Peter de Sève.

Naked Grandsanta

Grandsanta is intended to feel diminished, a big man who has shrunk, his clothes too hanging off him. But early in the development process I mentioned to Pete de Sève that I was finding it hard to decipher Grandsanta's body shape under these baggy clothes. By return came a delivery of these wonderfully funny, cheeky naked pictures of Grandsanta.

—S<small>ARAH</small> S<small>MITH</small>, <small>DIRECTOR/WRITER</small>

Grandsanta's Design

Grandsanta is the most colorful and funny character in the movie, in my opinion. Aside of the general challenge to make all the characters deliberately imperfect and quirky and also keep the Aardman spirit in the design (while not replicating literally the trademark Aardman stop-motion look), there were some specific challenges for Grandsanta: he had to be frail and small which posed the risks for him to look like a dwarf or an old elf. At the same time the audience had to be able to believe that once upon a time he was that real iconic Santa but just got really old . . . He is 136 years old in the movie! His face is very expressive and it was a struggle to shape his beard in a way that would give us the desired silhouette and yet, not intersect with his nose in animation. The CG modelers and the cloth & hair artists had to do numerous iterations and tests until we got the look and the functionality we needed while not limiting the expressiveness in the acting that Sarah expected.

—Evgeni Tomov, production designer

Just like Your Uncle Joe

Grandsanta says some of the most inappropriate things but the reason it works is that we all have someone like that in our family. You kind of go, "Oh yeah, there's Uncle Joe." You still love your Uncle Joe, but you know you can't take him anywhere. Like in most families, everyone wants to be together but everyone drives each other crazy.

—Chris Juen, producer

Assassinating Santa

The funniest character to me is Grandsanta who is 136 years old. We set out to make him an old person who behaves badly. Both Sarah and I had grandmothers who would say the most outrageous, un-PC, offensive things. But we still adored them.

Grandsanta is this guy who just says what everyone else is thinking. My favorite scene is during dinner when he is hassling Steve about being passed over for his promotion. He turns to him and says, "You're not going to get that job unless you knock him off." He's telling Steve he needs to assassinate Santa, his own father.

—Pete Baynham, screenwriter

ABOVE: Tim Watts.
RIGHT: Sculptures Evgeni Tomov.
OPPOSITE: Early concept drawing by Zébé.

Grandsanta is cranky and a nuisance but he and Arthur share something: an uncomplicated, deep, and profound commitment and enthusiasm for the idea of Christmas. He's the only one who can truly help Arthur.

—Bill Nighy

Mischievous Rascal

I think the Aardman "house style" is not so much an aesthetic as it is a comic sensibility. We didn't go for the googley eyes or wide mouths—what might be considered an Aardman look—but we did chase the Aardman sense of comedy. This gave us the freedom to be a little more edgy. It let us make Grandsanta such a mischievous rascal. He likes to get a rise out of people but it is always with a playful tone. Both Peter and Sarah's work in the past veers towards quite edgy comedy and the best example of that in our movie is Grandsanta.

—Alan Short, animation supervisor

ABOVE and RIGHT: Sergio Casa Castano.

ABOVE: Peter de Sève.
BELOW: Sergio Casa Castano.
ABOVE RIGHT: Barry Reynolds.

THE OLDEST REINDEER

Grandsanta's faithful old companion is the deer who led the sleigh way back in the old days when Grandanta himself was the traditional Santa in the original sleigh. Dasher is inspired by a springer spaniel I once had. They're great big dogs, but they like to climb right up on your knee and sit there, or lean their head heavily on your shoulder from the back seat of the car. We exhorted the animators not to treat the animals in the film anthropomorphically—they were never to have human expressions or behaviors. But this reindeer was to be as expressive as an animal can be; he was animated as a bright, but ancient, loving old dog. Pete de Sève nailed it in an early series of charming drawings (far left, top).

—SARAH SMITH, DIRECTOR/WRITER

Santa

voiced by Jim Broadbent

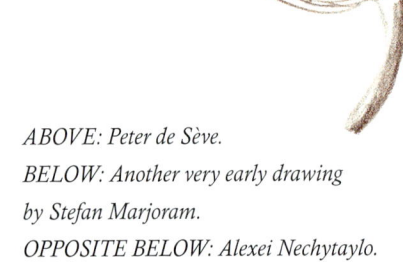

A big jolly, white-bearded man in a red suit, Santa (Malcolm) Claus XVIII is every inch the hero of Christmas. But in recent years, as the operation has grown more complicated, he's become more of a figurehead. He still delivers the presents as the General of his vast army of elves, but it's Steve who coordinates it all, even if dad seems a little oblivious to that fact. Truth be told, Santa's better at connecting with the children of the world than his own two sons. It's tradition that every Santa reigns for 70 years, and the time has come for this Santa to hand over the reins. But is he ready to retire? Being loved by billions of children worldwide can get a little addictive. And what's there to do in the North Pole when you're not Santa any more?

ABOVE: Peter de Sève.
BELOW: Another very early drawing by Stefan Marjoram.
OPPOSITE BELOW: Alexei Nechytaylo.

The Iconic Claus

Santa comes with so much expectation from the audience—he must be rotund and jolly with a white beard—that it is hard to find a specific original character in there. Pete de Sève drew him as a benign vague military type. Tim Watt's final Santa organized him to a pleasing tapered shape, with a face that could screw up into a high apple-cheeked smile, or droop to a confused hang-dog.

—SARAH SMITH, DIRECTOR/WRITER

> Here's to Me, doing an even better job next year!
> —SANTA

BEGGING YOUR PARDON, SIR BUT YOUR STANDING ON CAPT. TOMLINSIN, SIR.

Upper Management at Aardman

Every film that Aardman makes is totally unique. We were very excited when *Arthur Christmas* first came to us because we thought it was a great opportunity to explain to our families how Santa actually managed to do Christmas. Also Aardman really gravitated towards the characters that Pete created. A lot of times, in our film development, we begin by finding the personality of the characters. Our philosophy has always been that if we get the characters right, their world will follow.

Some of the characters in *Arthur Christmas* were clearly based on senior management at Aardman. Now, I am not at liberty to name names because my job would be on the line but, if you look at the way Santa acts, well, there is someone quite high up at Aardman who is quite like him.

—STEVE PEGRAM, PRODUCER

Jolly Santa

Santa has a kind of wide-eyed deer caught in the headlights look to him as he's not always quite in control of things. But as he's Santa, he also needed to look jolly and that involved the cheeks squashing up underneath the eyes when he smiled. I did a model at one point where one half of the face was stretched and the other squashed. Sarah urged me to cut and pull it around even further until we found something that satisfied those extremes.

—TIM WATTS, CHARACTER DESIGN ART DIRECTOR

ABOVE (left and right): Peter de Sève.
ABOVE (middle): Yves Barre.

Mrs. Santa
voiced by Imelda Staunton

I've just got to visit elf hospital, look over a treaty with Greenland and make 2 million more mince pies...

—Mrs. Santa

Mrs. Santa may have spent her whole life at the North Pole, raising her sons, educating the elves and baking two million mince pies on Christmas night, but we suspect that Steve's giant brain and calm demeanour came more from his mother than his father. Like the wives of most world leaders, Mrs. Santa is a highly intelligent, capable, caring woman forced to exist in her husband's shadow. But when it comes to the crucial moment when Santa has to step up and go back out into the world in order to do the right thing, it's Mrs. Santa coordinating things, using knowledge gleaned from decades of reading, studying and taking Internet classes in everything from global navigation to flying a microlight aircraft. Yes, she's off to help navigate the ship, save Christmas and bring along "a sweater for Arthur, Grandsanta's pills and some nice sweet tea."

RIGHT: Peter de Sève.

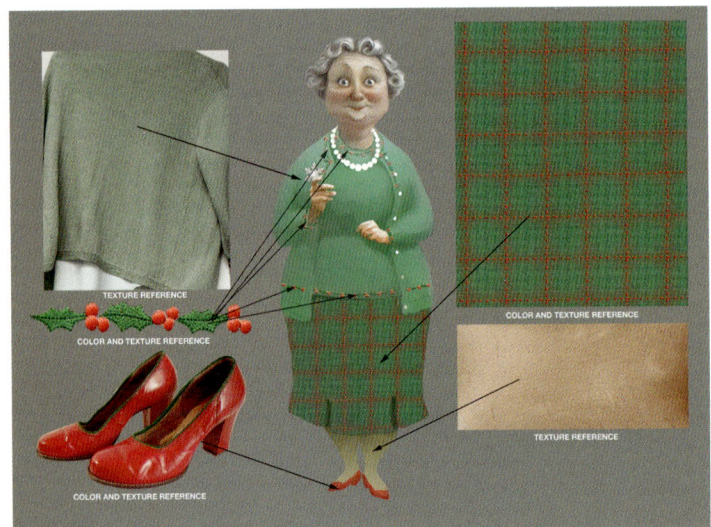
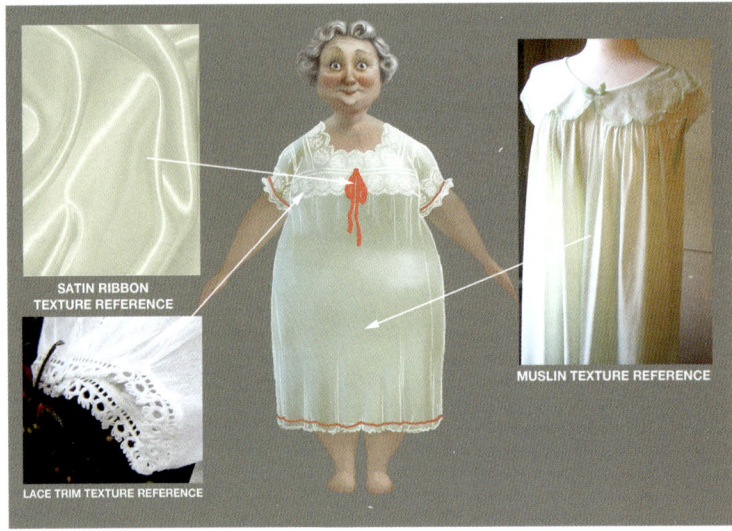

Mrs. Santa is a cross between the Queen and an Army wife.

—Sarah Smith, director/writer

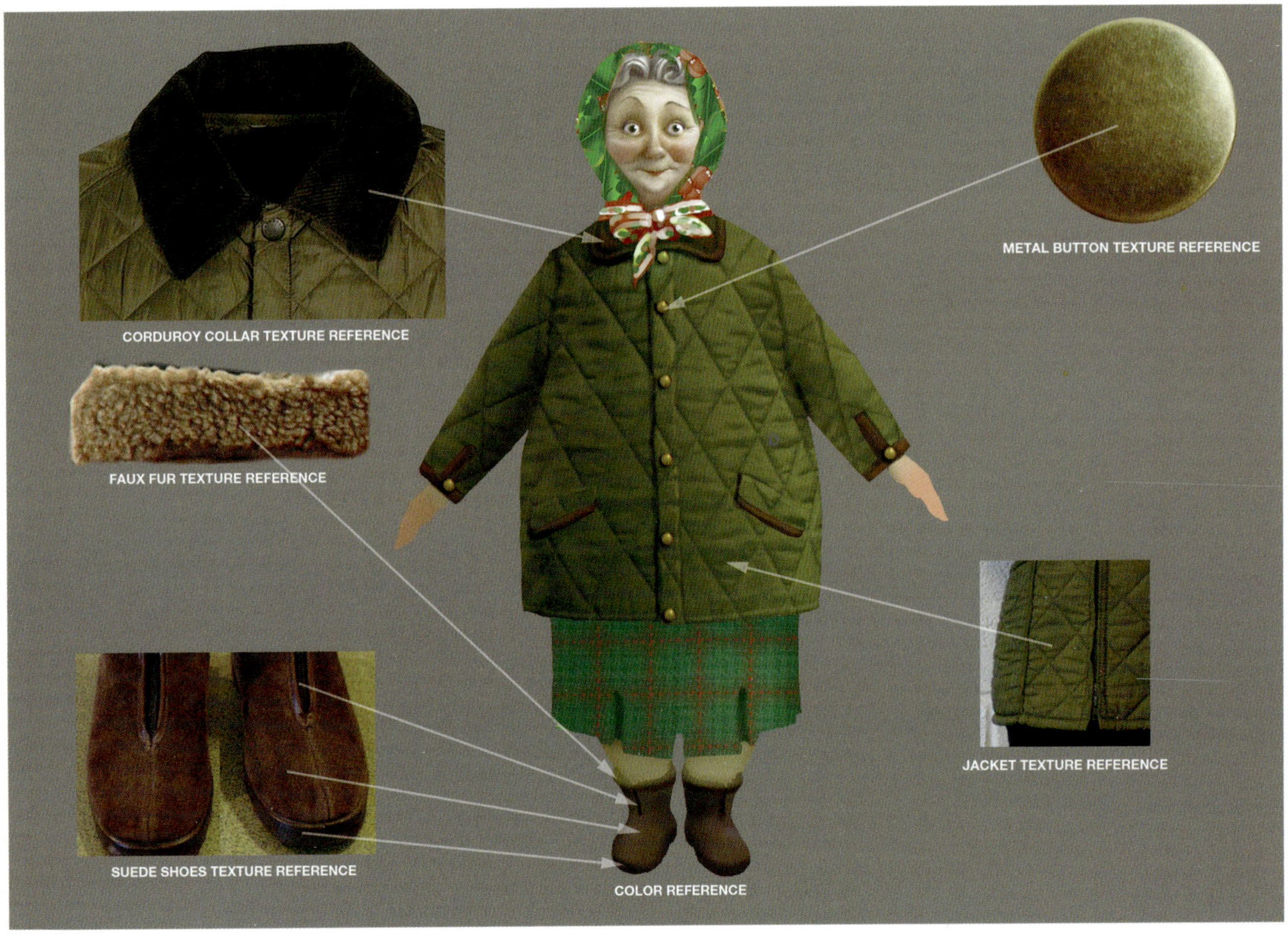

Mrs. Santa's Underwear

My main conversations with Tim Watts, the character art director, were about her underwear. This woman needs a spectacular foundation garment. The kind of thing the Queen wears, to keep her utterly securely held in and out at appropriate points. You could put her on a trampoline and NOTHING would move. She's large but utterly self-contained and dainty.

—SARAH SMITH, DIRECTOR/WRITER

Mrs. S to a T

If I hadn't been told that Imelda Staunton was to be the voice of Mrs. Santa, I would have used her as inspiration anyway. Mrs. S. needed to have not only a no-nonsense air about her but an elfin twinkle in her eye as well, which describes Staunton to a T.

—PETER DE SÈVE, CONCEPT CHARACTER DESIGNER

OPPOSITE: Alexei Nechytaylo.
ABOVE: Peter de Sève.
ABOVE RIGHT and RIGHT: Tim Watts.

Steve
voiced by Hugh Laurie

> Steve is incredibly cool and slightly in love with himself—the kind of character that doesn't quite get it. But Hugh completely gets it and gave us a beautiful and funny performance.
> —SARAH SMITH, DIRECTOR, CO-WRITER

Santa's oldest son Steve is the hereditary heir to the Claus reign. He's extremely qualified for the job, having introduced high-tech efficiency, military-style precision and the ultra high-performance S-1 sleigh ship. "If we all gave in to the Xmas spirit, there'd be chaos!" he says. Steve has dreamed of being Santa all his life; he's even redesigned the Santa suit into something more akin to Armani than Saint Nick. But Steve might still have a little catching up to do in the heart department.

BELOW LEFT: Peter de Sève.
BELOW RIGHT: Alexei Nechytaylo.

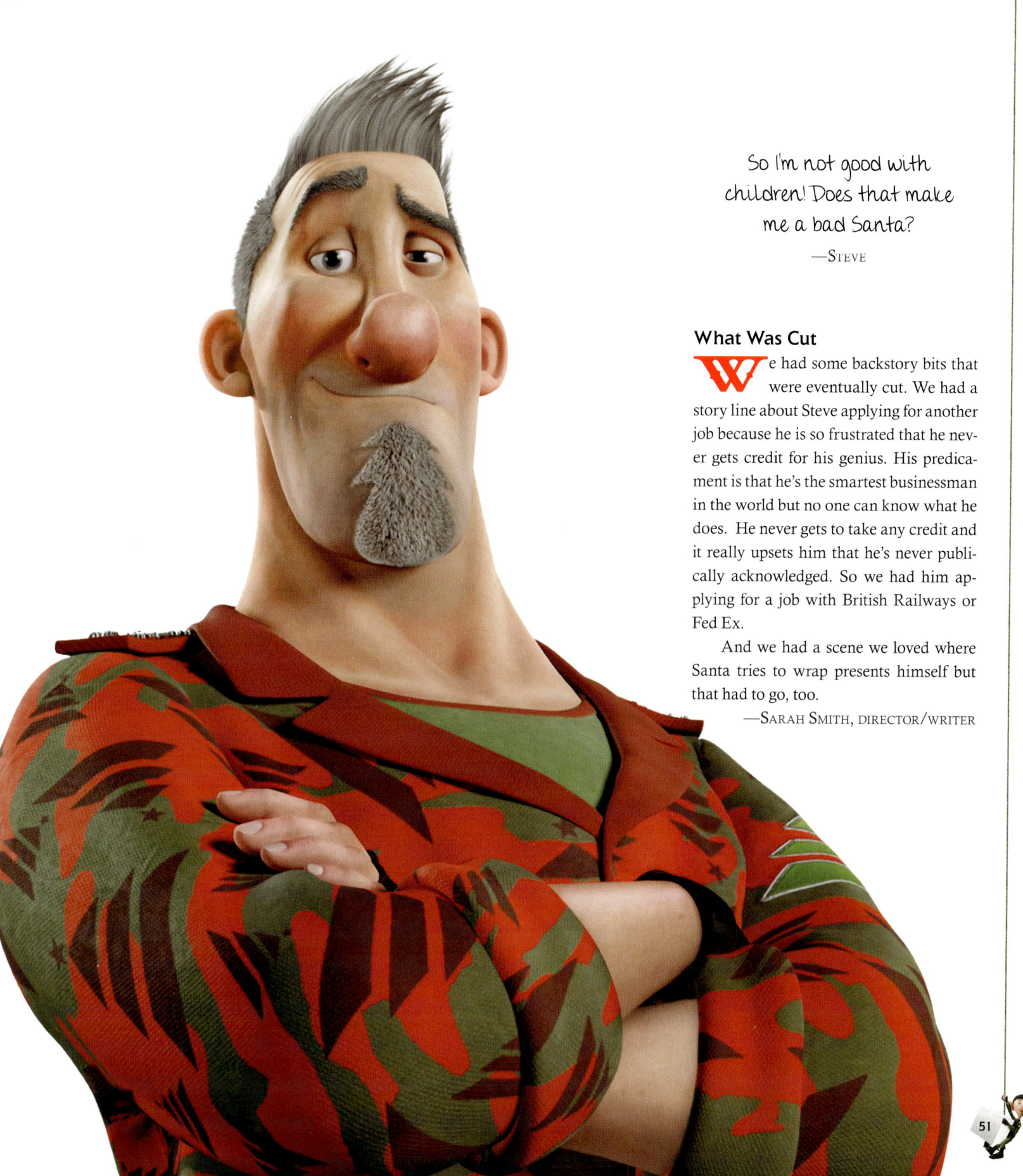

So I'm not good with children! Does that make me a bad Santa?

—STEVE

What Was Cut

We had some backstory bits that were eventually cut. We had a story line about Steve applying for another job because he is so frustrated that he never gets credit for his genius. His predicament is that he's the smartest businessman in the world but no one can know what he does. He never gets to take any credit and it really upsets him that he's never publically acknowledged. So we had him applying for a job with British Railways or Fed Ex.

And we had a scene we loved where Santa tries to wrap presents himself but that had to go, too.

—SARAH SMITH, DIRECTOR/WRITER

Alpha Male

Steve was largely Tim Watt's design. In his first incarnation he was edgy and heroic, the square-jawed, wide-shouldered alpha male. But as the Clauses were looked at as a family, it became clear that Steve was just a little too angular in the face, and some degree of rounding and softening was needed to show the family resemblance. Steve's suit, gloves and earpiece came from drawings by Zébé, based on the outfits of Formula One motor racing drivers.

—Sarah Smith, director/writer

OPPOSITE: Zébé.
ABOVE: Tim Watts.

LEFT: Barry Reynolds.
ABOVE and BELOW: Alexei Nechytaylo.

THE XMAS TREE MOTIF

Steve goes overboard with the Christmas tree motif. You see it in the camo pattern of his clothes, his goatee, even the soles of his shoes. Elves rappel down from the S-1 on stirrups in the shape of a Christmas tree. It tells you a lot about Steve's personality. It's all over the place!

—Alan Short, animation supervisor

BELOW LEFT: Tim Watts.
BELOW: Alexei Nechytaylo.

An Ant's-Eye View

Steve is a big guy and many times we give him less dimension to make him feel bigger. It's like the perspective of an ant looking up at us in real life; with their eyes really close together we probably look kind of flat to them. It's the same concept we are using to give Steve just a little bit less depth than anyone else. It helps to make him feel more dominating.

—Corey Turner, stereographer

Steve's Ambition

Steve's ambition would be to take a breakfast meeting with Bill Gates, to travel business class while being served champagne and to be on the cover of *The Economist*. He's never had that sort of recognition. He loves the whole Christmas operation because he manages to pull it off but he sort of wishes that somehow he could get credit for his genius. He is desperate to be Santa because he wants to be head of the organization. He kind of forgets that he's not that keen on children and he's not that into Christmas.

—Sarah Smith, director/writer

STEVE'S BEDROOM

What I love about the design of Steve's bedroom is this big curve that goes from the bed to the ceiling. In the real world it would be a very courageous design, difficult to build and expensive. I am very happy that it stayed in the movie because usually 9 out of 10 ideas are killed during production. The curved walls and the fancy bed are meant to show the extravaganza of Steve. The room is a funny mix of a rich kid's bedroom and some Asian Feng Shui. My work on this was based on the great story board sketches by Chris Pearn, so it's been a team effort, as always in film design.

—Till Nowak, digital set designer

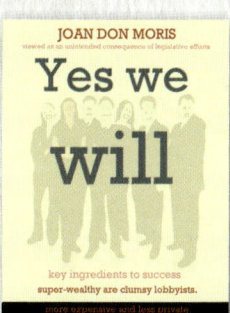

RIGHT: Alexei Nechytaylo, Jerry Loveland and Joseph Feinsilver.

Elves

I can wrap anything with three bits of sticky tape: THREE!
—Bryony

Bryony
voiced by Ashley Jensen

Elf Bryony Shelfley, Wrapping Operative Grade Three, is a lowly member of Santa's Giftwrap Battalion. A loyal, if somewhat manic foot soldier, Bryony is utterly obsessed with her job: Not called up for the field duty this year, Bryony served out the mission in Giftwrap Support where she wrapped 264,000 presents and can list every one of the 118 types of ribbon bows.

Over Eager to Please

Bryony's job is to help the Claus family and she is very keen to please, perhaps a bit over eager. She goes along on the mission and becomes the third comic member of the team. She has a very distinctive hairstyle and a ring in her eyebrow. Her look was inspired by a woman on the security staff here at the studio.

—Peter Lord, producer, Co-founder of Aardman

OPPOSITE: Drawings by Luis Grane.
ABOVE: Stephen Hanson.
BELOW: Bryony's HoHo 3000 displays 118 types of ribbon bows that she can create. Alexei Nechytaylo.

Wrong with the World

There are a lot of men in a movie about Santas! From early on we wanted a fun, feisty girl character—a stowaway elf. Bryony is an obsessive. One of my favorite lines from the movie which never made it was hers: "You know what's wrong with the world today? Printed bags. That's not wrapping!"

—Sarah Smith, director/writer

Peter

Peter is Steve's overenthusiastic, over-adoring right-hand elf, in charge of ensuring that his master's every need is satisfied, from prepping France for the big mission to getting him expresso. Peter idolizes Steve to a remarkable degree, to the point of giving him boxer shorts with a big "S" on them for Christmas.

> Don't worry, sir! Children are stupid. Either it won't know it got missed or it'll think it's been bad. It's a win win.
>
> —Peter

TEXTURE REFERENCE

TEXTURE REFERENCE

COLOR REFERENCE

MISSION CONTROL TROUSERS TEXTURE REUSE

LEFT and BELOW: Alexei Nechytaylo.
ABOVE: Barry Reynolds.
OPPOSITE: Luis Grane.

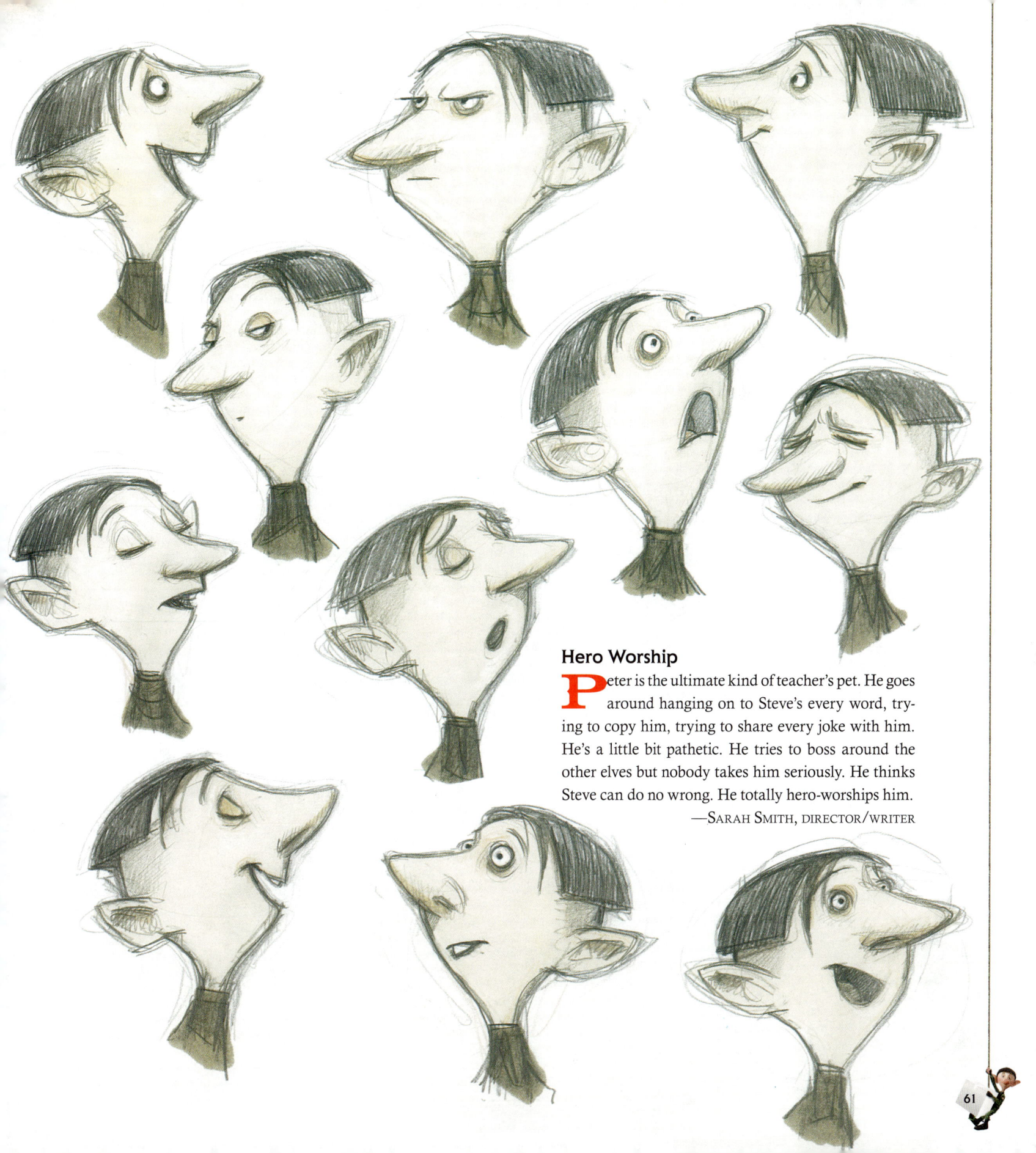

Hero Worship

Peter is the ultimate kind of teacher's pet. He goes around hanging on to Steve's every word, trying to copy him, trying to share every joke with him. He's a little bit pathetic. He tries to boss around the other elves but nobody takes him seriously. He thinks Steve can do no wrong. He totally hero-worships him.

—Sarah Smith, director/writer

Building A Million Elves

Stop frame and CG animation are two very different techniques but with both we try to capture the essence of developing very strong characters and telling a great story.

From the very start, we decided to do *Arthur Christmas* in CG animation, instead of stop frame, mainly because of the scale of the story. Everything about it smacks of CG. There are a lot of locations all around the world and that would have been really hard to accomplish in stop frame. Also, there are a million elves, which really can't be built as individual puppets in stop frame. The look has a very high-tech feel.

Also, things like creating ice are quite hard to do in stop frame. For all sorts of reasons, the designs just seemed to fit better into the CG milieu.

—David Sproxton, producer, Co-founder of Aardman

Stealthy, Acrobatic and Nimble

I knew that apart from looking like the elves we have always seen appear alongside Santa Claus, they also needed to have a kind of paramilitary twist to them, which opened up a lot of doors for me. They would have to be stealthy, acrobatic and nimble . . . but not too nimble. I liked to think of them as being very good at what they do, but not perfect. What fun would that be?

—Peter de Sève, concept character designer

> The elves are a cross between chickens and teenagers.
>
> —Sarah Smith, director/writer

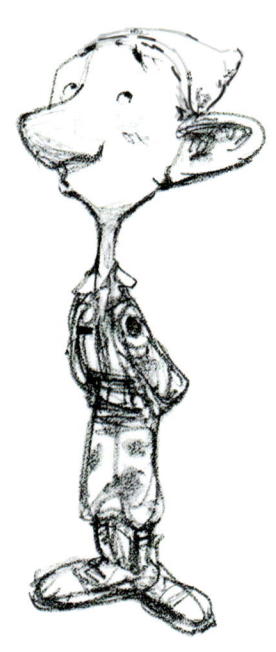

OPPOSITE and TOP: Very early concept drawings by Stefan Marjoram.
ABOVE: Peter de Sève. BELOW: Zébé.

Complete Idiots

You don't want this to be a purely sentimental look at Christmas without having some contrast. The elves take their work seriously to an outrageous level. They are a super slick, highly trained group like Marines or the S.A.S. They are not superhuman but they're agile and athletic acrobats. But when they aren't given orders or told what to do, they're complete idiots. At the drop of a hat, they think Christmas is falling apart and they panic. They go from being a totally supportive, well-oiled machine to thinking that their world is falling apart, and we play off of that contrast.

—ALAN SHORT, ANIMATION SUPERVISOR

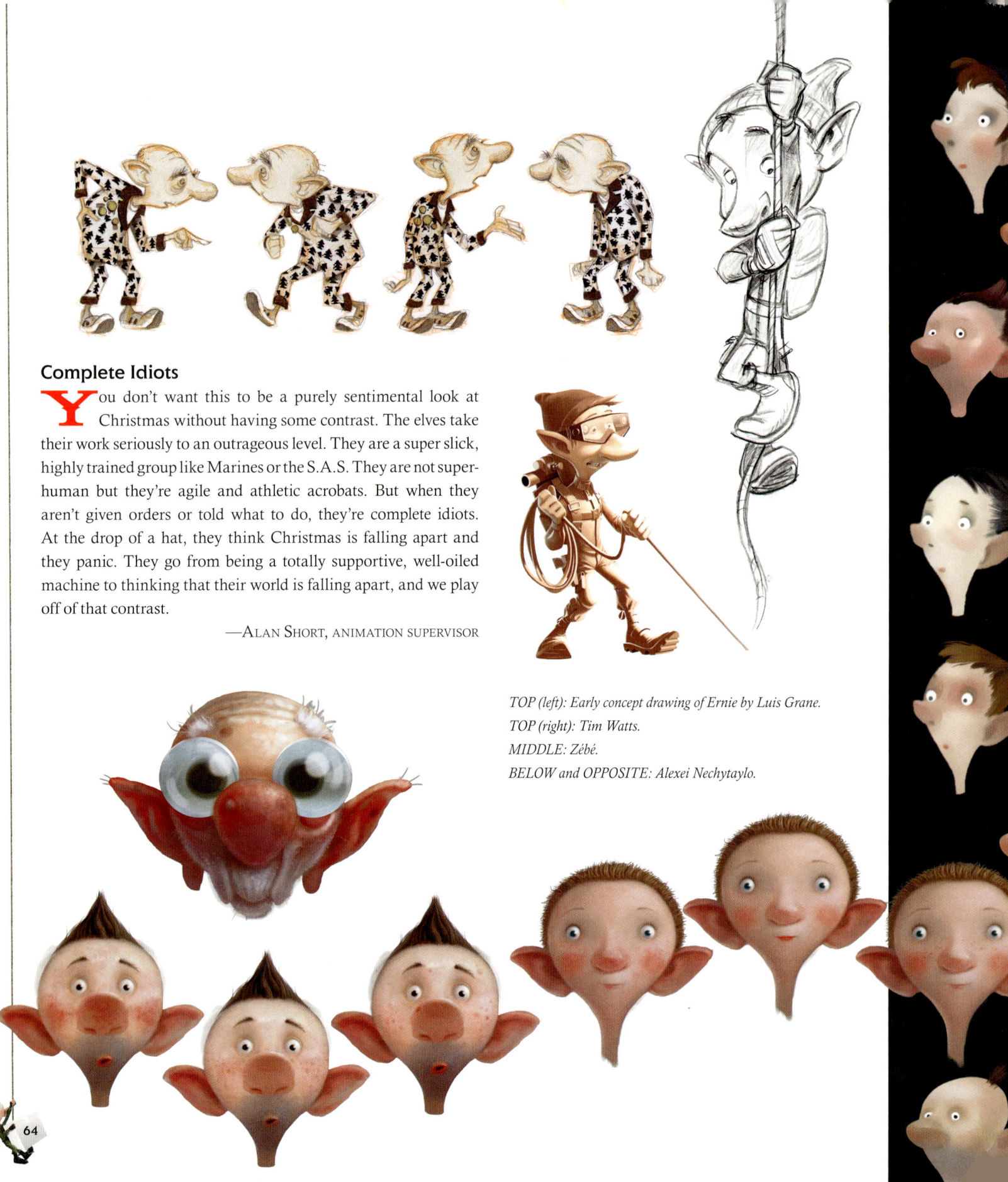

TOP (left): Early concept drawing of Ernie by Luis Grane.
TOP (right): Tim Watts.
MIDDLE: Zébé.
BELOW and OPPOSITE: Alexei Nechytaylo.

ELVES

The main imperative for the elves was that they should NOT look as they do in live-action Christmas movies as either miniature humans or dwarves in green tights. Other than that the field was open!

Pete de Sève started with a very eclectic range of body and head types. Pretty soon we fell for the lollipop look—big heads, pointy ears and noses, long skinny bodies.

The biggest problem they posed was for animation—many of them have such big heads and short arms they cannot do a handstand—which limits the acrobatics they can perform in the line of gift delivery duty.

The ranking and clothing system for the elves has its own very complex logic. Each one actually wears a badge showing rank and function within the mission. I wonder if any of these badges is ever seen on screen! I did become a hat fascist: "Too many red berets in this section! All beanies off in this scene, they've just got out of bed! That elf shouldn't have a blue shirt on!" It was slightly insane . . .

Sony's system of character variation suited these designs very well. They are simple but have a common "look." Alan Short's pass at posing the first set of these elves to be generated showed that many charming individuals could be created from the range of hairstyles, head and body shapes and skin tones in the variation system.

—Sarah Smith, director/writer

ABOVE: Peter de Sève
RIGHT: Alexei Nechytaylo and Sam Davis.

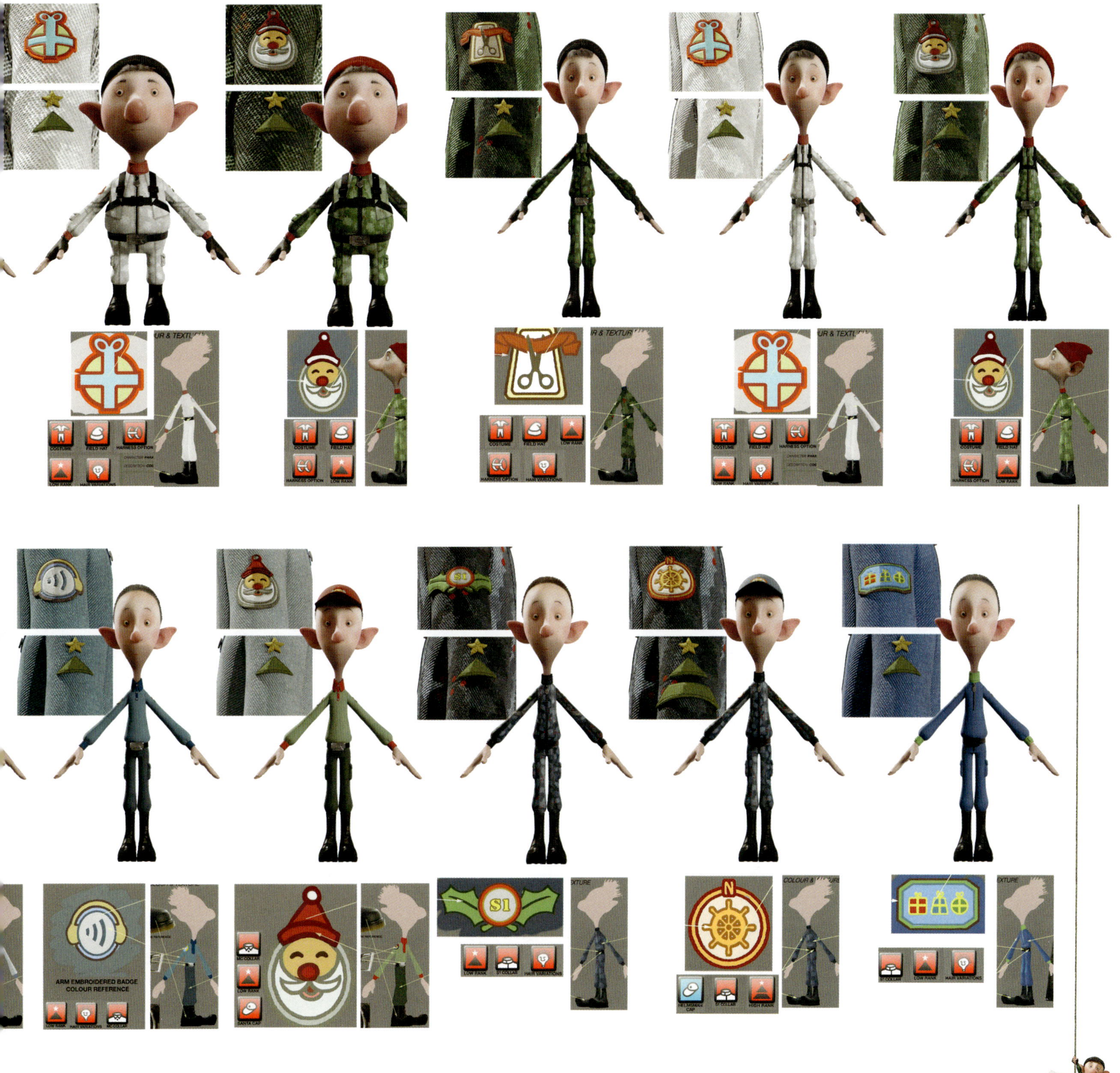
ARM EMBROIDERED BADGE
COLOUR REFERENCE
S1

STOCK-1NG COINS TOYS NUTS

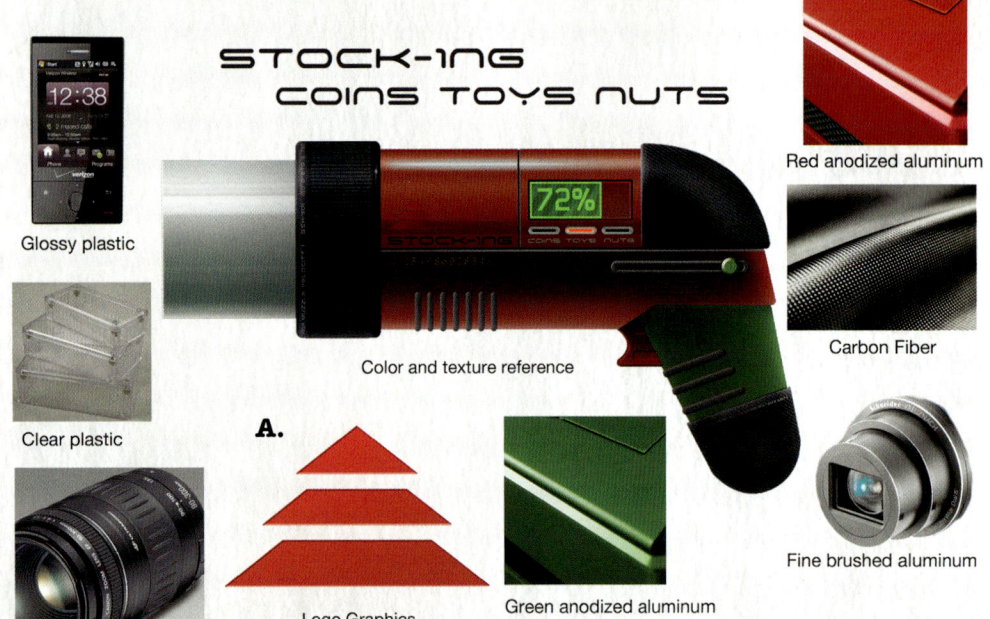

Glossy plastic
Clear plastic
Rubber
A.
Color and texture reference
Logo Graphics
Red anodized aluminum
Carbon Fiber
Fine brushed aluminum
Green anodized aluminum

"STOCK-1NG" STOCKING GUN
For use by MISSION ELVES, ALL RANKS

Pump-action, repeating. Can fill whole stocking in 1.14 seconds. NEVER fire at own face or child. This may result in rapid discharge of candy canes, chocolate coins and small toys at the target and make a big mess. Replenish on S-1, Level 5. **A.**

NLB – NEVER LEAVE BEHIND! Children could replace contents with water, tennis balls or small pets.

WRIST-MOUNTED DROP COUNTER
For use by MISSION ELVES, ALL RANKS

For continuously updated 'Drop Time': number of seconds per household. Mission average 18.346 seconds for house of 2.698 children. **B.**

Night Vision INFO-SPEX
For use by MISSION ELVES, ALL RANKS

Darkness-enabled goggles. Inner lens displays mission updates, child data and residential hazards, e.g. squeaky steps, aggressive pets and suspicious kids with cameras. **C.**

WARNING Use in daylight may result in dizziness and banging into things.

B.

C.

PET-STOP 1000 ANIMAL TREAT RIFLE
For use by MISSION ELVES, ALL RANKS

Fires species-appropriate treats into mouths of noisy house pets. DO NOT USE on animals below 2 inches in length! Pat these creatures to achieve silence. For oversize pets, e.g. horse, bear or above, liaise with your Team Leader. Settings: PARROT, PONY, DOG, CAT, RABBIT, and GOLDFISH.

Personal Consumption from Pet-Stop during mission IS FORBIDDEN. A chocolate coin and festive energy bar are in your backpack.

NIGHT-CUT X1225 LASER-GUIDED SCISSORS
For use by GIFTWRAP BATTALION ONLY

Power-assisted, laser-aided scissors for covert wrapping, repairs and rewraps in the field. DO NOT RUN with this item. Non-mission use, e.g. cutting hair, uniform repairs and dividing up pizza STRICTLY FORBIDDEN.

SHOULDER-MOUNTED TAPE GUN
For use by WRAPPING BATTALION ONLY.

High velocity precision tape dispensing pistol for wrapping, repairs and rewraps in the field. Features tape-coming-off-roll silencer for child-proximity situations and electronic thing for finding the end.

HoPAD.
Currently used by HEAD OF POLAR OPERATIONS STEVEN S CLAUS *ONLY*!

No information available at this time.

(When you click on this, Steve's voice says "Don't touch that! Put it back!" etc.)

There's Always Time for a Bow

Every team of three field elves carries a multitude of SAS-style gadgets and gizmos to help them get in and out of houses and deliver their presents in the 18.4 second drop time. Designed to look sleek and cool yet simple and witty, the team behind them looked at everything from military hardware to wrapping and stationery kits!

—ALAN SHORT, ANIMATION SUPERVISOR

THESE PAGES: Alexei Nechytaylo.
FOLLOWING PAGES: Stephen Hanson.

Gadgets

D.

SNOW GRENADE
For use by MISSION ELVES, ALL RANKS

For covert camouflage and security camera disorientation. When detonated, equivalent to 16.76 snowmen of High-Whiteness Polar Snow. DO NOT explode near angry polar bears or in a colleague's bunk as a practical joke. **D.**

CHOMP-500.
VACUUM/MUNCHING DEVICE
For use by MISSION ELVES, ALL RANKS

For precision biting/chomping/sucking up food & beverages left out for Santa and reindeer. **E.**

Settings: Santa (Cookie/Mince Pie/Shoe full of rice) and Reindeer (Carrot).

"SUCKER X-15"
BACK-MOUNTED 'LEAVOUT' TANKS
For use by MISSION ELVES, ALL RANKS

For use with CHOMP-500 VACUUM/MUNCHING DEVICE.

For containment/disposal of food and beverages left out for Santa and reindeer. Capacity: 1.3 gallons of festive gunk. ONLY DISPOSE OF CONTENTS ABOARD S-1!

GRAPPLESUCK G-6
BUILDING ACCESS GUN
For use by MISSION ELVES, ALL RANKS

For access to high windows. High tensile cable connected to rubber suction cup with sticking power of 10,000 MegaSucks. NEVER fire at moving object such as car, train, airplane or rampaging elephant.

KIDSCAN 500
For use by MISSION ELVES,
(HOUSE ENTRY SPECIALISTS)

Back-of-hand Mounted Behavior Sensor. Scans target children for Naughty/Nice score through year. Wireless connection dictates STOCK-1NG Stocking Filler gun delivery amount.

F.

HOHO3000
(Handheld Operational
and Homing Organiser)
For use by ALL NORTH POLE PERSONNEL
(Except Arthur and Grandsanta)

100 Million Terabyte Personal Comms Unit. For communications, navigation, emergency alerts ('Elf down,' 'Waker', 'Total Rewrap Required'), data storage, texting your friends and remotely checking the temperature of a roasting turkey. Must be turned off for S-1 launch and landing. **F.**

X-DROP ELF BACKPACK
For use by MISSION ELVES, ALL RANKS

Lightweight Mission Backpack. Contains: Compass, Emergency Magic Dust Capsule, Spare pet treats (see Pet-Stop 1000), First Aid kit, Giftwrap Repair Kit (Giftwrap Battalion only), vacuum-packed socks, spare earplugs, mittens, Emergency Mistletoe, and 'Elf Down' instructions in case of stranding. **G.**

CHOMP 500: VACUUM & MUNCHING DEVICE

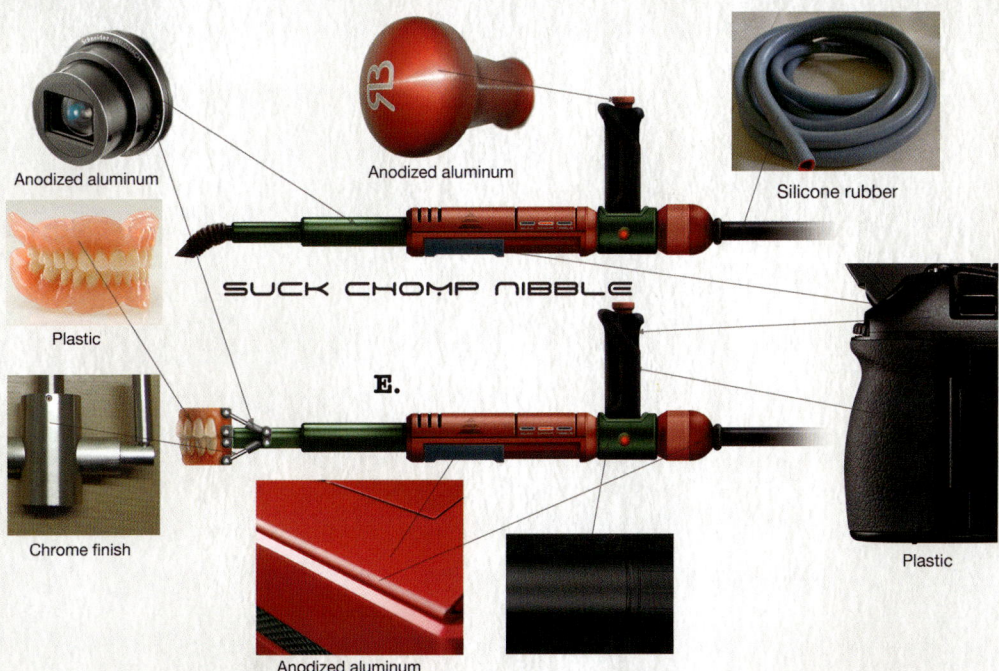

G.

Part 2
"How Does He Do It?"
December 24, 11:58. Aarhus, Eastern Denmark

BEAT BOARDS

Beat Boards are done very early on, several years before the movie goes into production. These drawings support all the major moments in the film and give us a sense of what the film could look like. Sarah showed us these boards in Bristol and they were instrumental in creating enthusiasm for the film's concept.

It is always interesting to look back on these drawings. As you can see, the characters became much more refined during the course of production. Although the look changed quite dramatically—as it always does from this stage—the power, charm and humor of the story was there for us from the very start.

—Bob Osher, President, Sony Pictures Digital Productions

Like a Comic Strip

Beat Boards are kind of like a comic strip, with each panel showing a key moment or event. What I enjoy most about doing beat boards is that they are usually done quite early on in the process, often before much of the design work has been started, and that allows you quite a lot of freedom artistically. I also like the challenge of trying to find that one, single image that sums up an entire sequence.

—Adam Cootes, story artist

THIS PAGE: Beat boards by Adam Cootes.

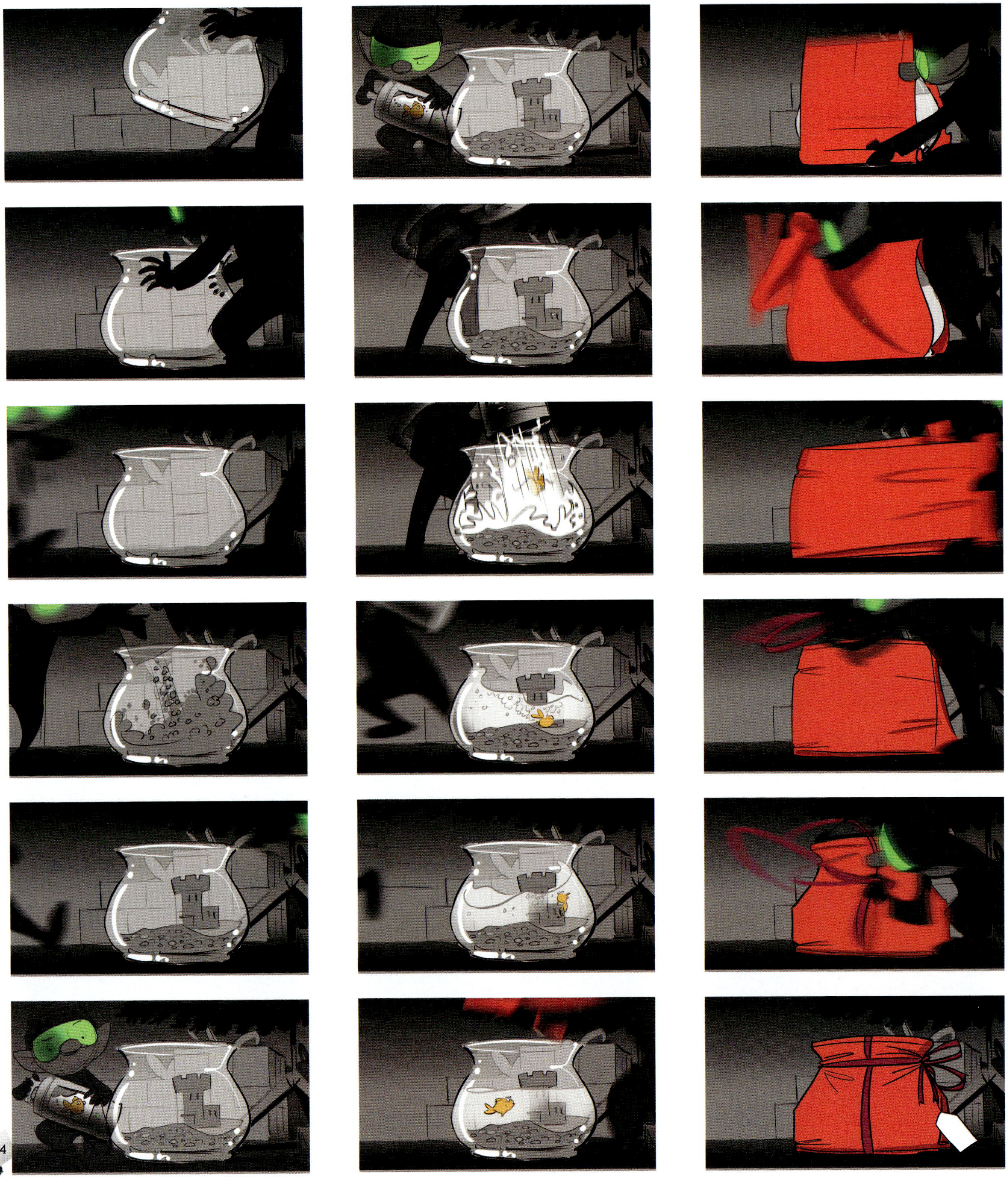

What the Elves Can Do

The Delivery Elf reaches the bed of a sleeping child. She passes an electronic scanner over his face; 71% Nice. The elf takes her stocking-filler gun—small toys, chocolate coins and a satsuma pump in.

Other elves spot bowls of rice pudding with a sign "For Santa." With hoses they suck it into a back-mouthed bottle.

On a staircase a sleeping child has a camera fixed on the Christmas tree hoping to get a picture. A craft elf snaps a picture of the empty room holding it in front of the camera while the other elves deliver the gifts.

A wrapped airplane glides under a tree. An elf pops up the floor board under a sleeping dog to make the drop. A wrapped space hopper gets bounced on an elf.

Gifts of all shapes and sizes appear under trees and in stockings: Telescope! Piggy bank! Rocking horse! Train set! Bouncy house! Robot! Goldfish! Garden gnome!

A Delivery Elf spots her target, a stocking, and leaps gymnastically at incredible speed through an impossible maze of paper chains!

An elf scans the face of a sleeping child: "Naughty." He quickly scans his own face: "Nice," and fills the stocking.

Storyboards convey a rough idea of the visual sequence of the story and are created very early in script development. Storyboard art by Adam Cootes and Kris Pearn.

Color Keys

From Film Noir

The color script is the heart of the film and maps the emotional charge of each sequence. It may look fairly abstract but it sets the mood, color and ambiance of the film. All the work is based on these color concepts.

This movie had so many locations, and each one had its own challenge. Snow and ice are always problematic to create though Sony is really good whenever we needed to show water; they have the technology to do that really well. Perhaps the single most challenging element was that most of the movie plays out at night and includes a number of very dark scenes. I think, at first, we made the movie too dark, so we had to pull back. We went from a kind of film noir look to a day-for-night one.

—Alexei Nechytaylo, art director

I am a traditionally trained painter but all of my color keys are painted in the computer. I can do more paintings in less time as well as easily making any last-minute changes to them.

Color Keys are created once we move into actual production. These paintings are more than just showing where the light in a scene is coming from. They should also help support the story by providing appropriate color and mood.

—Michael Kurinsky, art department, color keys

THESE PAGES: Evgeni Tomov and Mickael Kurinsky.

Lighting Keys

Lighting or Color Keys are an important stage in the development of an animated film. The samples on this page show how much light can affect the emotional landscape of a scene. Note, for example, the warm glow and cozy feeling of the image (above) of Arthur reading Gwen's letter, which is in the opening of the film. Then look at how the mood of the room changes in the image (top right) in the scene where Arthur is despondent that Gwen will not get her promised Christmas gift. The room is the same but changing the lighting creates an entirely different feeling.

Cozy, Imperfect and Well-Lit

We wanted to maintain the Aardman style, not so much the stop-motion style, but the Aardman feel which I can only describe as cozy. It took us a long time to figure out. We didn't want our characters to look like they were made out of clay, yet we wanted that imperfection you get from clay characters. The realistic lighting also plays into the look. So you have imperfect cozy characters in very real cinematic lighting. The look is more film-oriented than computer-generated.

The texture and realism of Arthur is probably the most ambitious we've ever done. The amount of detail in the look really pushed the envelope. You feel like you could pick something up and it would be real.

—Chris Juen, co-producer

Heart of Christmas

This shot is where we find Arthur reading and replying to Gwen's letter and promising her the Twinkle bike. In terms of lighting this shot it is in direct contrast to the opening shot of the film. It's intimate, colorful and warm; this is where the heart of Christmas works—with festive reds and Arthur with his garish Christmas sweater. In number, the shot is just shy of 1000 frames. Each frame took approximately 25 hours to render its final image.

—David Satchwell, CG supervisor

ABOVE (right images): Michael Kurinsky. All other images on these two pages are Lighting Keys meant to give direction of light and light, mood and emotion of the story. OPPOSITE: Michael Kurinsky and Evgeni Tomov.

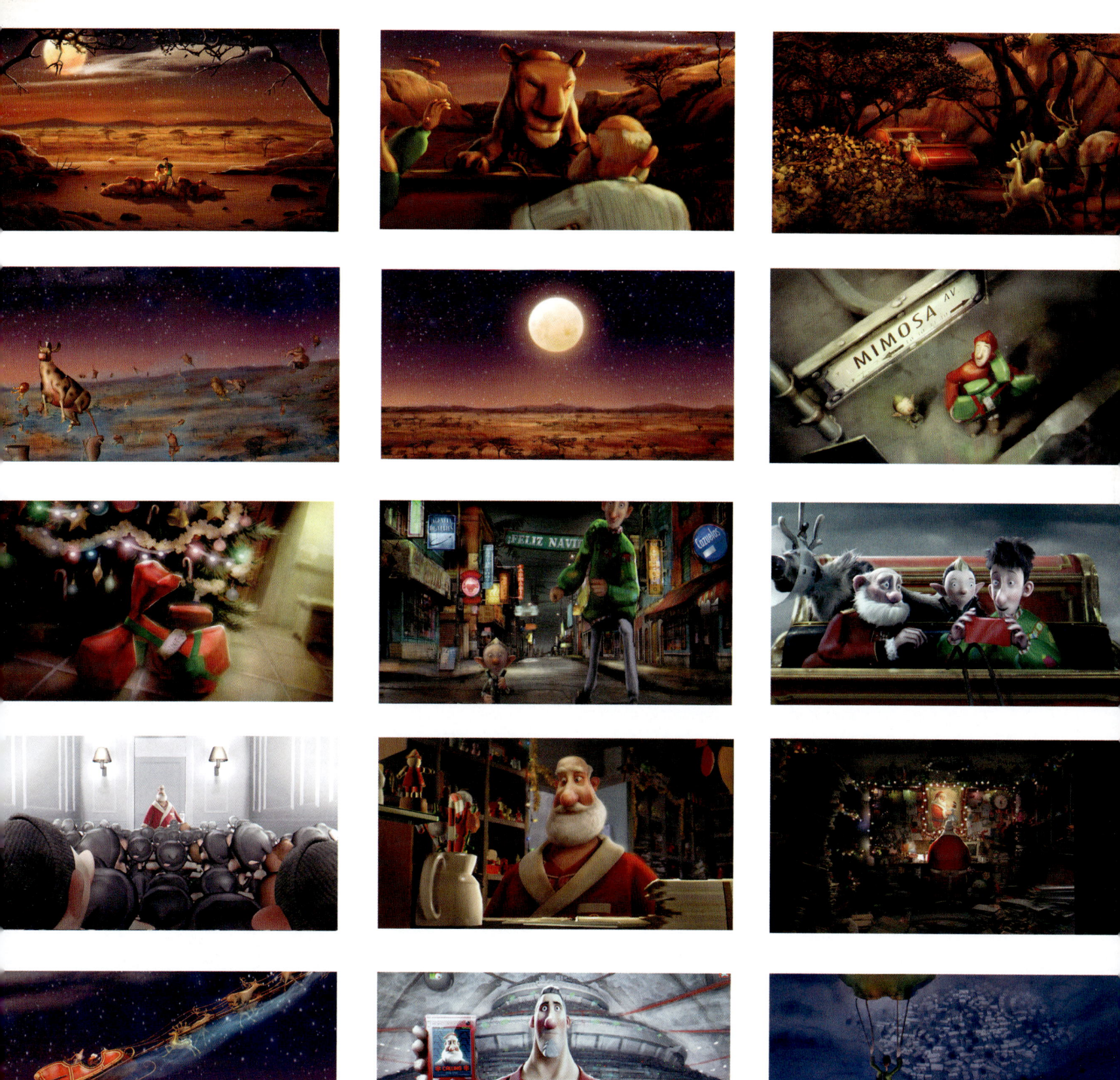

Production Paintings

More Real than Real Life

We set out to do something very particular—to create an Aardman CG film. I didn't really know what that meant when we started, other than that the characters needed to feel like they could only come from Aardman; that they were somehow British and they belonged to the Aardman family without in any way borrowing from the character design principles that come from stop frame like *Wallace and Gromit*.

The idea for the look of the film was based on the idea of the story itself, which had to feel like it was a true world that every child has imagined. Everything in the movie is meant to feel real so, for example, our technology is never sci-fi. The gift-wrapping machines look like Hewlett Packard could build them. The conveyer belts in Mission Control resemble the sorting system used by Amazon or FedEx. It is a real world with a heightened magical feeling. I compare it to the night you go to sleep on Christmas Eve; everything is the same as the night before except there seems to be something sparkly and special about the world.

We didn't borrow a particular look or style or genre from any previous film, so we had a fairly scary process of character and art development. This movie is ridiculously overambitious in the number of sets and characters it requires. It's a road movie that literally goes around the world.

—Sarah Smith, director/writer

Multipurpose Paintings

The Production Paintings have a multiple purpose: early in the design process they help define the visual style of the film. Producers and studio executives love them as they show as close as possible the final look of the movie. They help the director to visualize and define the feel of a particular scene and check if the chosen color palette and lighting deliver the needed emotion. The Production Paintings are as well very useful visual reference for the texture artists, lighters and compositors in the CG production. It is definitely fun for an artist to create Production Paintings and I indeed enjoyed painting some of them!

—Evgeni Tomov, production designer

Production paintings by Olivier Adam, Evgeni Tomov, and Stephen Hanson.
FOLLOWING PAGES: Stephen Hanson.

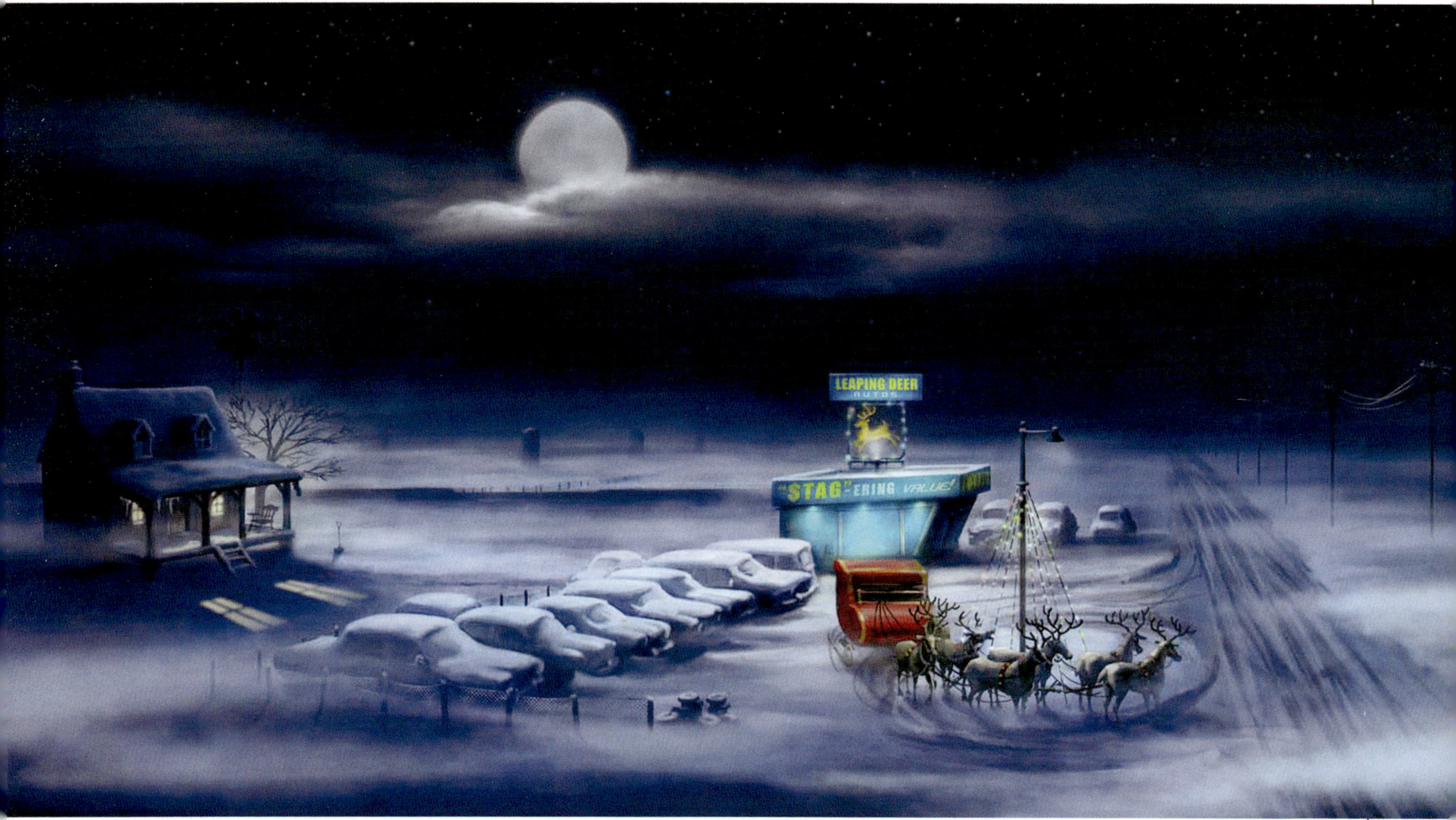

LEAPING DEER
"STAG"-ERING VALUE!

AGENCIA DE VIAJES
¡FELIZ NAVIDAD!
Golosinas
Médico
Doña Olga
El Cuaderno
Cazuelas
Luces

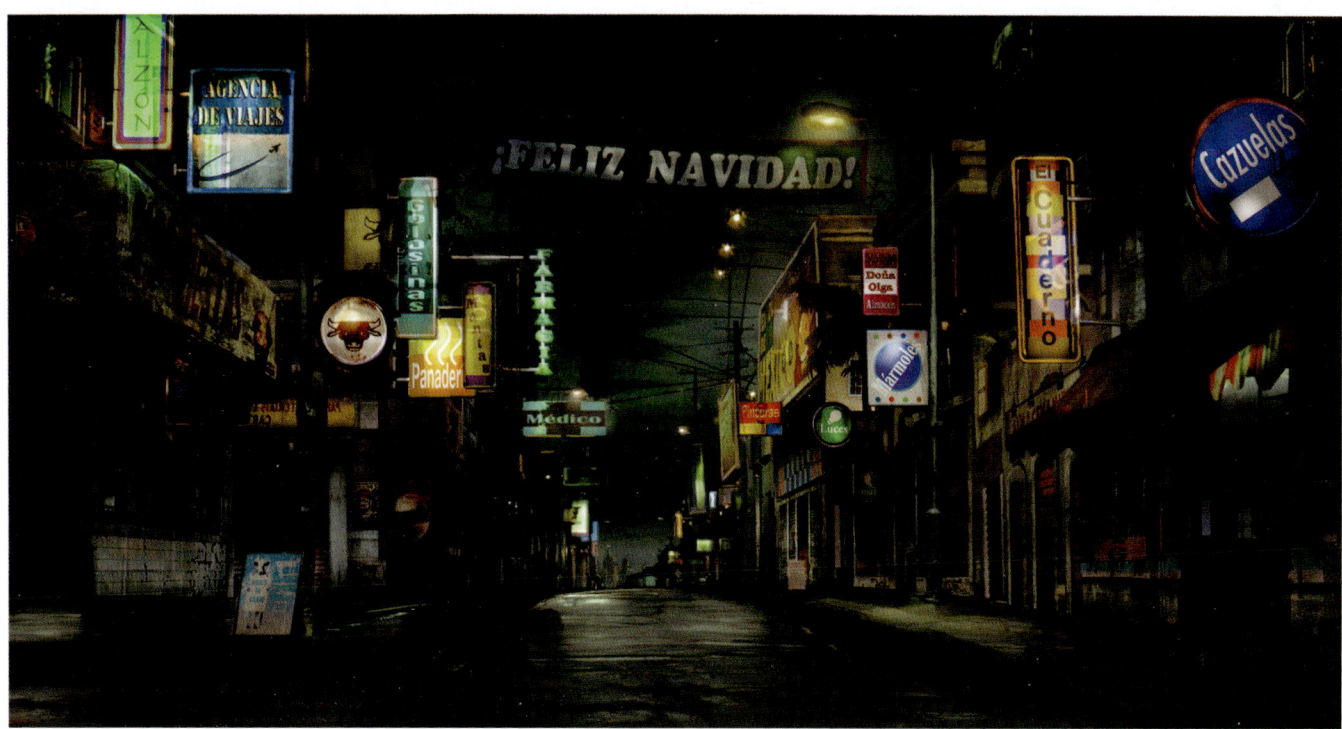

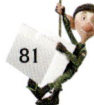

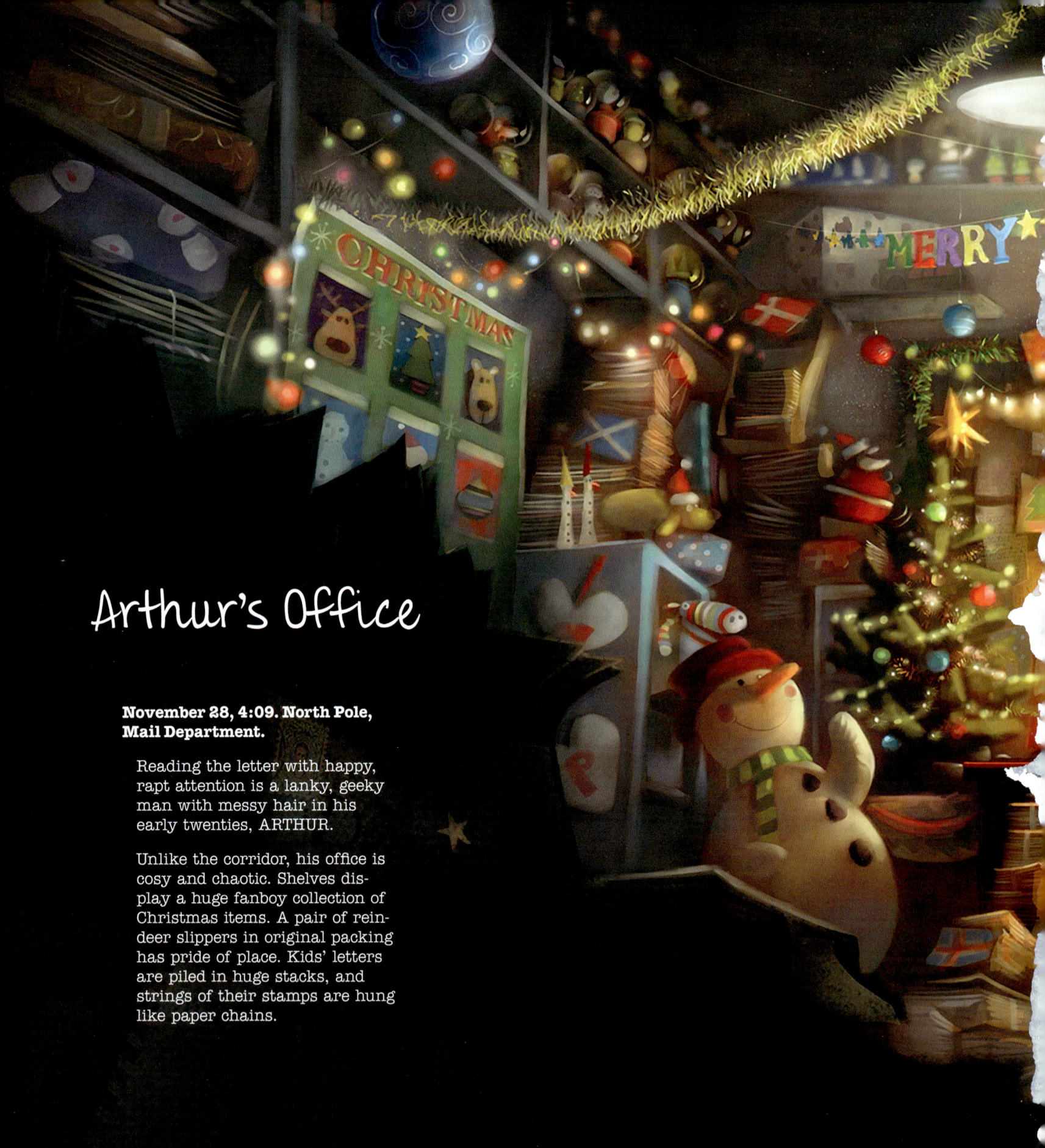

Arthur's Office

November 28, 4:09. North Pole, Mail Department.

Reading the letter with happy, rapt attention is a lanky, geeky man with messy hair in his early twenties, ARTHUR.

Unlike the corridor, his office is cosy and chaotic. Shelves display a huge fanboy collection of Christmas items. A pair of reindeer slippers in original packing has pride of place. Kids' letters are piled in huge stacks, and strings of their stamps are hung like paper chains.

The World Inside the North Pole

Letters vs. Emails

Arthur loves the letters from the kids but if Steve had his way, the letters would all be on email, which might be his plan for the future anyway. Arthur loves the physical tangible letters and the kid's drawings. He is hugely into all that.

—Pete Baynham, screenwriter

Christmas All Year Long

Arthur encapsulates the spirit of Christmas. He lives for it. Under Steve's leadership, Christmas has evolved into a rational, logical business like any huge corporation. Arthur, however, is still trying to hold on to the idea of the holiday and maintain a child's desire to believe in Santa. This is the conflict established early in the film.

Meanwhile, here in Bristol, it's been Christmas every day for years. We had Christmas decorations and a tree set up for the holidays and those are still here in the middle of summer. I think the team must be a little disoriented when they walk into the office.

—David Sproxton, producer, Co-founder of Aardman

LEFT (above): Evgeni Tomov.
LEFT: Stamps by Alexei Nechytaylo and Sam Davis.
OPPOSITE (bottom): Book covers by Stephen Hanson.
ABOVE: Bjorn-Erik Aschim.
BELOW: Olivier Adam.

In Love with the Holiday Spirit

From the very start of the film, we want you to know that Arthur is completely in love with the idea of Christmas. He adores everything about the holiday. So his office is a shrine to Santa and we made it look like it is literally overflowing with the Christmas spirit. It is all meant to show his child-like wonder and willingness to give into the spirit of the season. Soon we will discover that he is the only person in his family who feels this way.

—Bob Osher, president, Sony Pictures Digital Productions

Family Dinner

Dinner Scene

Everyone can relate to the dinner scene because we've all been there. The scene sets up the family dynamic that is going to carry us through the story. We see that Santa himself is past his prime but won't admit it or let go of his alpha status. We see that Grandsanta is obsolete. We see Steve, the next obvious Santa in line, has almost no emotion when it comes to what he's actually doing for the kids. And we see that Arthur is the only one hanging on to all the best things about Christmas. He just wants his family to all get along for one night and they can't even do that. They argue about a board game! And then we see Mrs. Santa is the real backbone of the family keeping it all together.

—Donnie Long, head of story

Symbolic Decorum

In this sequence we played with a minimum of decorum, almost a feeling of emptiness. We used the architectural structure (molding and doors) to increase the symmetry throughout the different shot axis. I offered to add a big painting of two reindeer fighting for leadership of the herd. This painting was on the wall behind Santa as a caricatural mimic of what was happening in the room: the fight between Steve and Grandsanta. In addition to this idea, we added a few more elements as symbols attached to each character: the heater behind Steve (warm/red color), the old ceramic Santa clock behind Grandsanta (the past), the cheap, sad Christmas tree behind Arthur (the only Christmas spirit in the room), the melting Santa candle behind Santa (end of an era), and the tea set and boiling water container behind Mrs. Santa (a lady's job as Grandsanta would say).

—Oliver Adam, environment art director

TOP: Stephen Hanson and Alexei Nechytaylo.
ABOVE LEFT: Alexei Nechytaylo.
LEFT: Stephen Hanson and Evgeni Tomov.

4:43 AM: North Pole Residential Headquarters

ARTHUR
What do you get if you eat Christmas decorations? Tinsilitis! (big honking laugh) Isn't this the best bit of Christmas?

ARTHUR
Mum! Are you okay?

MRS SANTA
Polar bear dear. Attacked me on the ice. Good job I did that online survival course, or it'd be one less for turkey this year.

GRANDSANTA
Christmas has gone right down the rodney hole! You're a postman with a spaceship!

STEVE
Postman with— My S-1 festivized the world at one thousand eight hundred and sixty times the speed of sound!

GRANDSANTA
Christmas 1941, World War 2, I did the whole thing with six reindeer and a drunken elf! I was shot at Arthur! Took twelve direct hits, lost *three* reindeer!

ABOVE and BELOW: Olivier Adam.

GRANDSANTA
D'you know Arthur . . . *there is a way!*

ARTHUR
It's impossible.

GRANDSANTA
They used to say it was impossible to teach women to read! Follow me.

"Hello, Evie . . . "

The old sleigh barn itself was both easy and difficult to design. It's in very traditional animation territory in terms of look, with its chunky beams, large and bold wood grain, etc. This made it instantly gettable and appealing—but there was a concern that it somehow belonged to another movie. How would it feel to see characters walk from Mission Control into this set?

There were two solutions. Firstly, Alexei's and the digital team's beautiful textures, extremely detailed, tactile and well observed, unite the look of all the enivronments. And secondly, the set is governed by the same idea—*it could be true*. It is not just beautiful and romantic, it is full of practical details. Old-fashioned tools, rusty canisters of magic dust, sleigh pre-flight checklists, the ancient map of the Clauses and trusty brass sextant, right down to the chimney lube and elf-extractor elf lube for delivery problems, are designed to convince that this is how it *would have been done* in the old days.

—S<small>ARAH</small> S<small>MITH</small>, <small>DIRECTOR/WRITER</small>

Least Suited to the Task

The most moving scene to me as an audience member is when Arthur and Grandsanta decide to deliver the misplaced gift to Gwen themselves. I responded to that scene because it personalized this impersonal world. The world around us is constantly reducing us to a statistic and here you see the characters reject that concept. Gwen is not a number, not a statistic, but a little girl with a name and an address. It doesn't matter to Arthur and Grandsanta that they're the least suited people to the task, they're going to try and do it anyway, because it's the right thing to do. The characters that were best suited to the task gave up. So this frail old man and this clumsy boy are going to go ahead and remind us what Christmas is all about.

—D<small>ONNIE</small> L<small>ONG</small>, <small>HEAD OF STORY</small>

LEFT and ABOVE: Evgeni Tomov.
BELOW: Michael Kurinsky.

Old Sleigh Barn

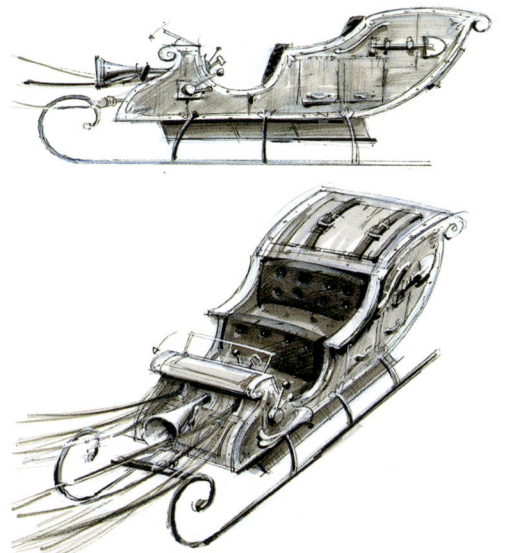

The Original Sleigh

To me the sleigh is the most beautiful thing in the movie. The textures are gorgeous—you want to reach out and touch it, as Arthur does. The glow of the bonnet is modeled on the lacquered wood of a cello, the burnished brass and worn leather of the seat are taken from vintage cars and fire engines.

In particular I love the dashboard with all its "bells and whistles." The design team laid out all the controls, then myself and Peter Baynham invented retrospectively what all the levers could do. We enjoyed the camouflage options (pigeons, shop, whale), but my personal favorites are the individual switches marked "reindeer pairs" and the HPS (Hooves Per Second) handle, to be cranked up in an emergency!

—Sarah Smith, director/writer

LEFT: Two of the very first drawings of the old sleigh by Evgeni Tomov.
BELOW: Alexei Nechytaylo.

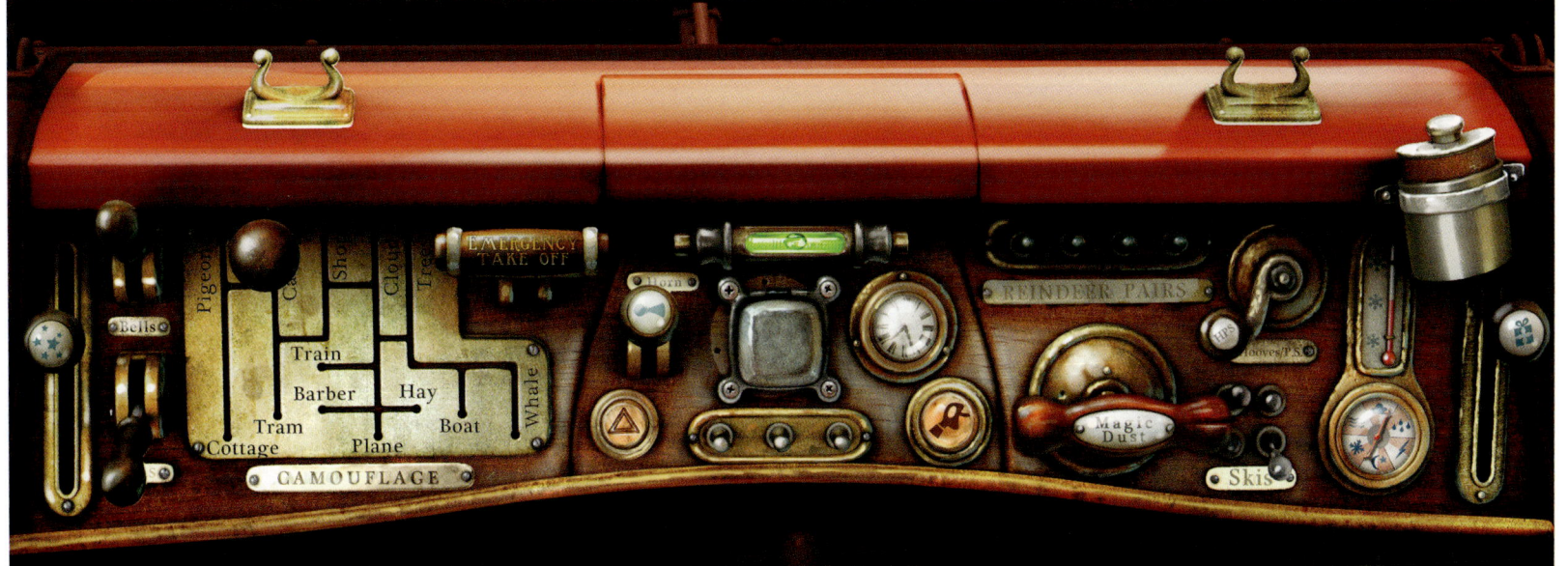

ARTHUR
Icelandic birch, Artic Balsa, built in 1845, able to reach 50,000 MPH at a height of 40,000 feet!

OLD VS. NEW SLEIGH

The film recreates the dichotomy of two worlds: the old world with the old sleigh and the hyper-techno world of the S-1. So everything we did was to play up on the contrast between those two worlds. The S-1 was always about scale; it is city-size and holds enough elves to work an entire city in one stop. Inside, it's a completely operational system. Outside, we focused on making it look super high-tech. Grandsanta's old sleigh was all about beauty. We wanted it to look custom-made with shiny metal and carved wood. Nothing on the old sleigh is fabricated, everything is handmade.

—Doug Ikeler, VFX supervisor

Old Sleigh in Its Glory

The scenes in which we are introduced to the beautifully polished and rich, deeply reflective surfaces of the old sleigh were some of the first on the movie to be fully animated and rendered; we were all just as impressed as Arthur to see it for the first time in its full glory!

—Seamus Malone, animation lead

OPPOSITE (top): Evgeni Tomov;
(below) Alexei Nechytaylo.
THIS PAGE: Alexei Nechytaylo, Stephen Hanson, Sam Davis, Barry Reynolds.

Two Parallel Worlds

This movie wants to re-explain Christmas but not lose the spirit of the holiday. We show two parallel worlds. We show the modern, high-tech, almost militaristic world that is led by Steve. It is efficient and spectacular but maybe a little cold. Grumpy Grandsanta represents the past with his old sleigh and the reindeer kept in the stable. Between those two worlds is Arthur who just loves Christmas and only cares that it is perfect for the children.

These two themes of the old and the new interweave in various ways. We literally cut between Mission Control, which is like Houston on steroids, and the old sleigh, which is made of birch and brass with a steam-punk vibe, and those furry reindeers gathering across the night sky.

—Peter Lord, Producer, Co-founder of Aardman

Christmas the New Way
(Dear Santa, How Do You Do It?)

If the audience were to believe "It Could Be True," we had to work out, for real, how Christmas really COULD be done in a night. No fudge, what would it ACTUALLY take?

We did crazy maths: How many kids are there in the world, how many celebrate Christmas, average number of kids per household; ten hours of night to fly round the world, of which flying time five hours; Santa's field army is one million strong, working in teams of three. 330,000 teams . . . We worked it all out and came up with the figure of 18.4 seconds per team per household. We worked out size and flying speed for the S-1 (the only rule here is that one mustn't predicate that it can fly faster than the speed of light since that is scientifically impossible).

It was important that the technology should not appear sci-fi; it needed to look true and believable and contemporary, so an audience would feel, "Of COURSE, that's what they use!" The design brief asked, what would it look like if the Pentagon took over delivering Christmas? Combined with Hewlett Packard, NASA, Amazon, UPS and Apple? We used to have a scene in which Santa tried to wrap his gifts for the family in a wrapping machine. The machine was designed to resemble a giant office photocopier in which you could select the pattern on the paper and the type of bow, etc. I'm sad we never made this machine!

And then we needed to stylize the look of our monitors, buttons, chairs and consoles to bring them into an animated world where our characters could walk. We were trying to find middle ground between the simplified style of *Wall-E* and the high-tech cool of *Minority Report*.

—SARAH SMITH, DIRECTOR/WRITER

OPPOSITE: Beat board by Adam Cootes.
ABOVE: Color key by Alexei Nechytaylo.

Mission Control

Our Crazy Techno Person

A lot of our designs in Mission Control were designed by Till Nowak, a German designer. He designs, builds, textures and models in 3D, he animates with camera shots. He built his version of Mission Control and submitted his work in 3D, not drawings. He did a complete throwaway model that had everything in it. And we set a large team of people to recreate it. The scene needed a crazy techno person in order to design such a technology set.

—SARAH SMITH, DIRECTOR/WRITER

Almost Before It Existed

I got on board of the project almost before it existed. I met Sarah Smith in France in 2006 after she had seen my short film, *Delivery*. She was planning to work on *The Pirates* and scouted me for that. In 2008 before Sony gave the green light I was involved for a couple of months in preparing the pitch and working with the very early concepts for *Arthur Christmas*. It was only a team of about five people in Bristol. I worked on Mission Control, the design of the S-1, the bridge of S-1, the dispatch room with the conveyor belts, Steve's bedroom, the S-1 docking bay, and a few of the smaller sets like UNFITA and the Toronto airport tower.

The design directive I received from my briefing with Sarah early in 2008 was that Mission Control should be the Dr. Strangelove war room meets NASA, times 100. It was meant to be very technology and look functional, but also be on a massive scale. Scale was the word I was hearing over and over for months; at one point I didn't want to hear that word anymore. I received concepts from other artists who put 100, 500 or maybe 1,000 elves into Mission Control. I took over and Sarah told me to make this bigger than anyone could imagine. So I did. I put in 15,000 elves. Then Ravi (Ravinder Kundi) built a digital mock-up based on Evgeni's concept that defined the Christmas tree structure and the final proportions of the set. I remember tons of sketches from Evgeni and Olivier that brought in key ideas on the way to the final design.

—TILL NOWAK, DIGITAL SET DESIGNER

OPPOSITE (above): Till Nowak.
OPPOSITE (below) and ABOVE: Production illustrations by Alexei Nechytaylo.

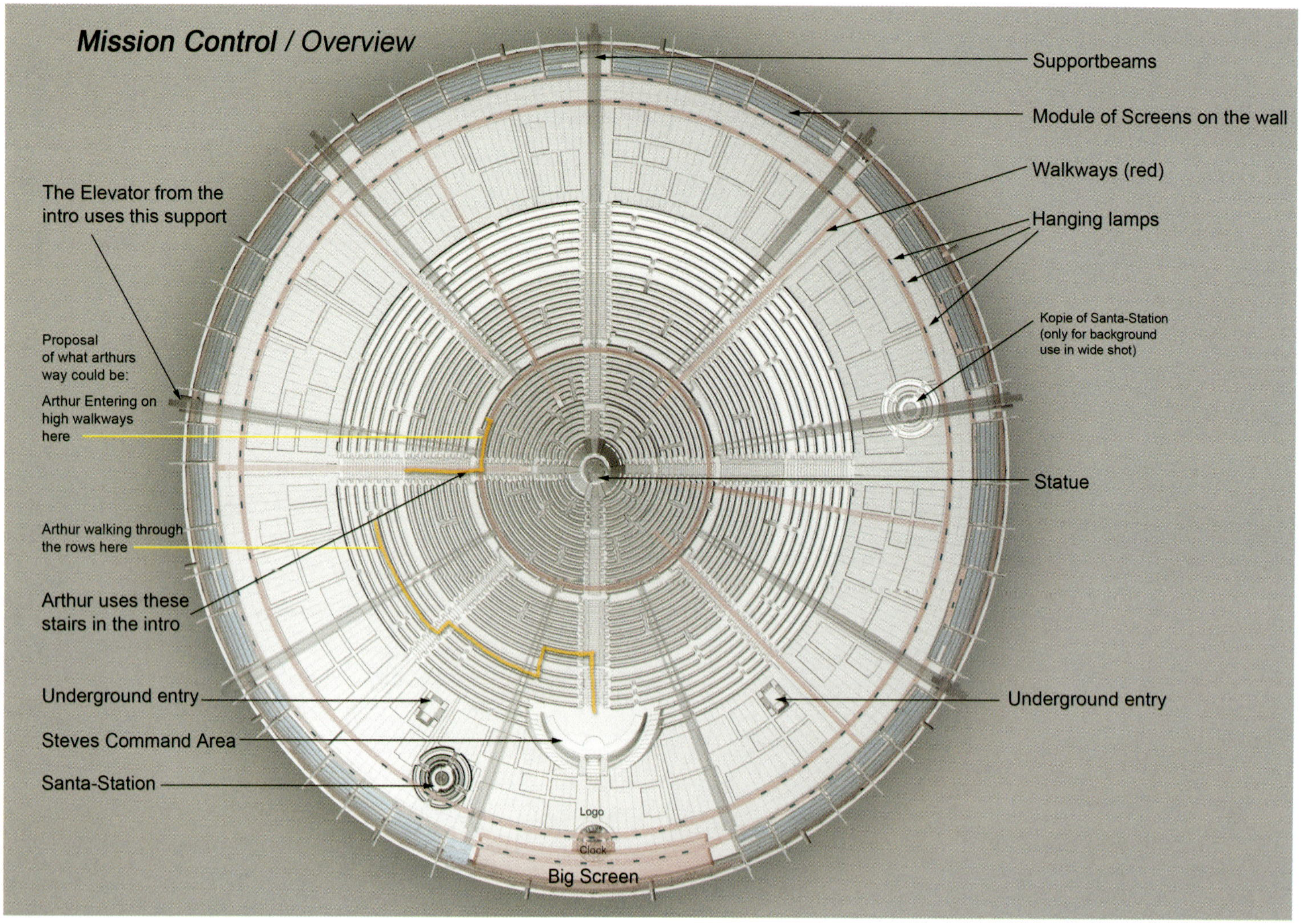

Mission Control / Overview

- Supportbeams
- Module of Screens on the wall
- Walkways (red)
- Hanging lamps
- The Elevator from the intro uses this support
- Proposal of what arthurs way could be: Arthur Entering on high walkways here
- Kopie of Santa-Station (only for background use in wide shot)
- Statue
- Arthur walking through the rows here
- Arthur uses these stairs in the intro
- Underground entry
- Steves Command Area
- Santa-Station
- Underground entry
- Logo
- Clock
- Big Screen

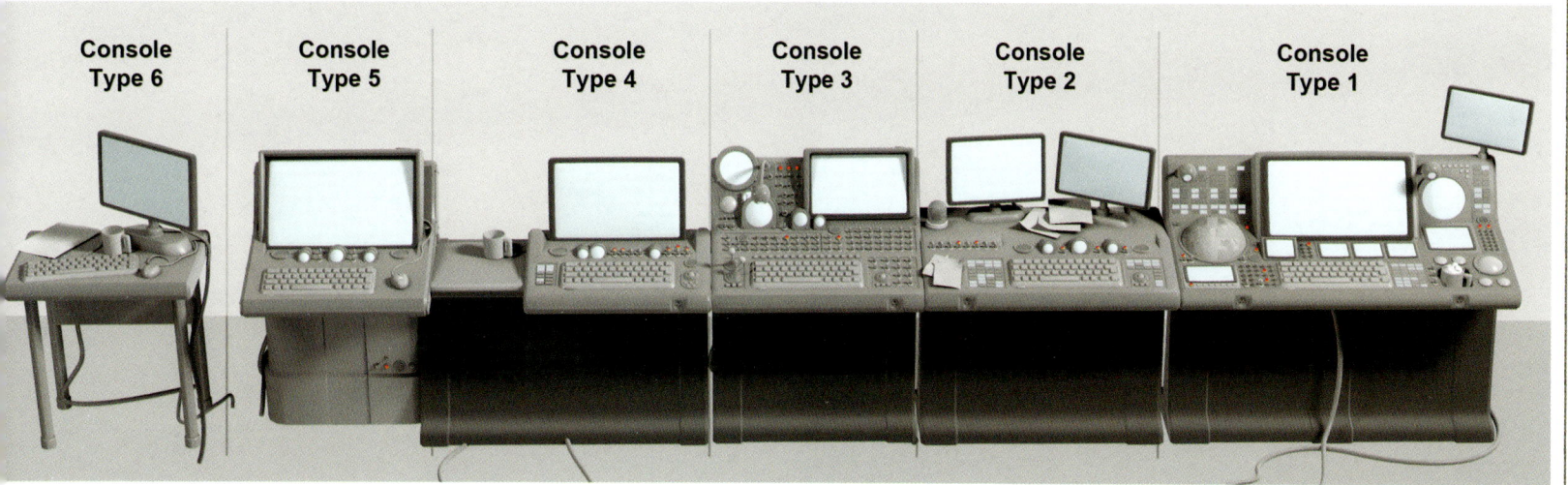

Funny Cup Holders

Mission Control is not realistic in terms of proportions. From far away, the computer terminals look like NASA but up close everything is a little clumsy and out of proportion. Every detail has minimal thickness so every border or edge is a little thicker and rounder than reality and has this cartoony style. It is also chaotic and funny in the details. Close up you can see that the elves have funny cup holders for marshmallows swimming in hot chocolate. On the S-1, there are pinball games, joysticks, espresso makers, record players and old telephones.

The bridge set actually had the most transformations. We had an automatic retractable red carpet and air bags and oxygen masks falling from the ceiling.

On this kind of scale, the challenge is to duplicate things without making them look duplicated. For example, there are tons of buttons on the consoles and one of my most difficult tasks was to arrange them. When you have straight lines, it's easy to duplicate but with round surfaces you can't easily use the automatic ways of duplication. All the positioning becomes irregular. The buttons were combined with six different types of computer terminals for the 15,000 elves. The consoles are made in ways that they can be combined to look random. However, the consoles on the bridge of the S-1 are round so duplicating elements on curved lines involves a gigantic amount of work. It is interesting that the big things were not the problem, it was the small details that took so much time and effort.

—TILL NOWAK, DIGITAL SET DESIGNER

All illustrations by Till Nowak.

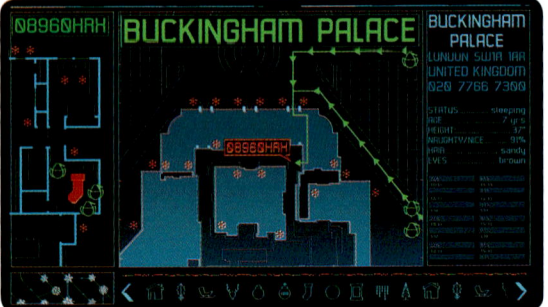

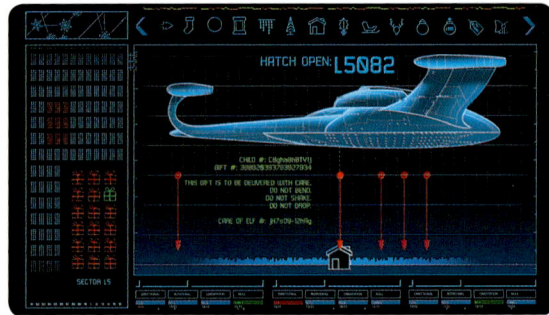

Motion Graphics

We needed an entire team of people to handle the scope of motion graphics on this film. We would be looking at a sequence of shots, and suddenly you would realize that hidden in the background was a screen with a witty comment, or some story point that only the keenest viewer would catch. Or, we would spend moments of a review calculating the time that would need to be set on a clock so that it matched the actual time that it would be in a certain country as the characters were working their way to Gwen's house.

—Mandy Tankenson, Digital Producer

On Second Viewing

The Motion Graphics in this movie are often integral to the story or play out specific gags. There are many sequences in the film where the entire scene is just a wall of screens displaying Elf technology and requiring a huge amount of artwork to be produced. We wanted to keep it light and humorous without losing the hi-tech look. So although some of the screen graphics play seriously, others are actually quite ridiculous on closer inspection. Charts monitoring Santa's cookie consumption, jolly meters, naughty/nice graphs, escape routes for Santa on the blueprints of children's houses, etc. I think this is a film the kids will see every year and each viewing will introduce them to a different layer of detail. They may not notice the first time they see it, but they are likely to on a second or third viewing.

—Alexei Nechytaylo, Art Director

All these motion graphics were designed by Alexei Nechytaylo and Evan Parsons.

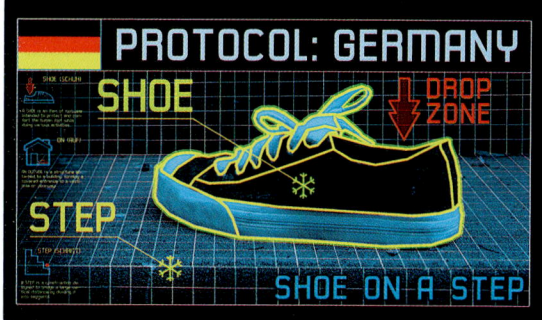

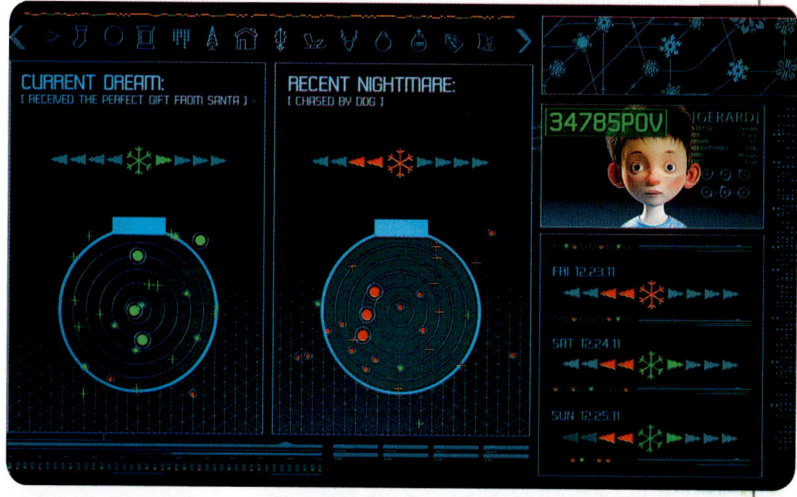

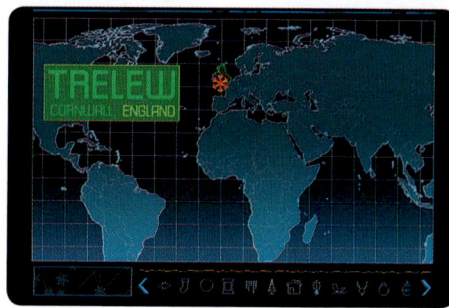
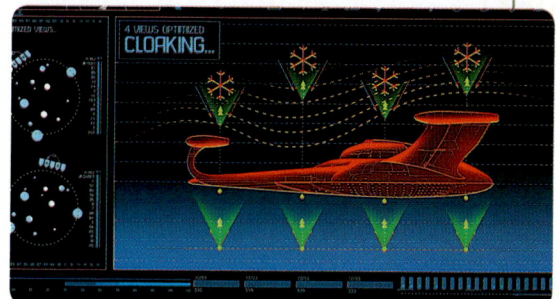

The S-1

S-1 SLEIGHSHIP SPECIFICATIONS

BUILT: 2008
MISSIONS TO DATE: 2

General

WIDTH: 1.16 miles
LENGTH: 2.08 miles
SPEED: 0.92 million miles per hour.
POWER: 15.22 trillion watts RP (Reindeerpower)
PROPULSION SYSTEM: STRICTLY CLASSIFIED (except to Clauses and Elves above Level 12.) Hacking this information is Level 1 Naughty and WILL RESULT IN LOSS OF PRESENTS!
CARBON EMISSIONS: 0.000000000000000000000000 0000000015 g per 1,000 miles.
CAMOUFLAGE SYSTEM: K-MELION X 1000 "Video Skin" enveloping craft projects any environment onto itself, rendering craft 100% invisible
COLOR (at rest, non-stealth conditions): Festiva Red Metallic Finish.

Personnel Capacity

ELVES: 1,000,023
CLAUSES: 5

Hold Capacity

PRESENTS: 2,000,000,000.
STOCKING FILLER (chocolate coins, candy canes, small toys, oranges): 121,000,000 metric tons.

Miscellaneous

BATHROOMS: 62,103.
COFFEE MACHINES: 1
AIRBAGS: YES
REAR WINDOW DEFOGGER.
USB PORT with smartphone connectivity.
TIME TO WASH: 3,876 Elf Hours.

LEFT: Alexei Nechytaylo.

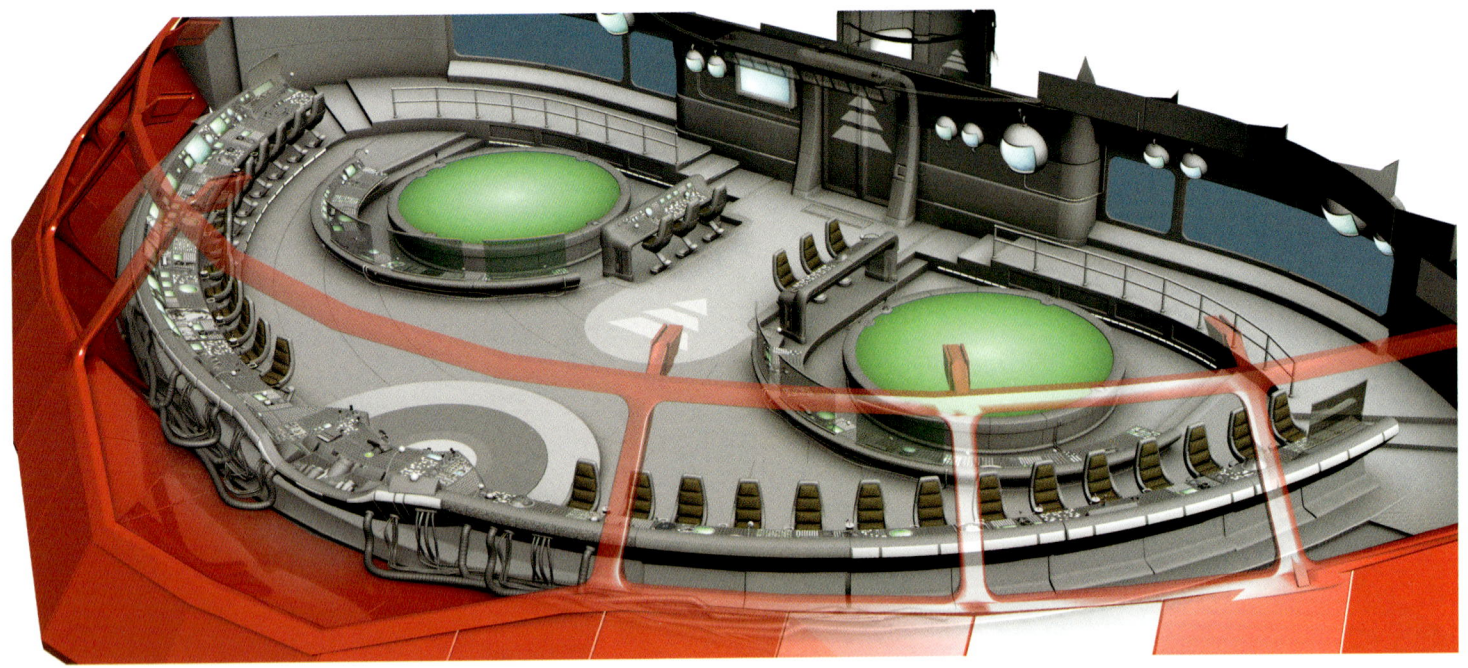

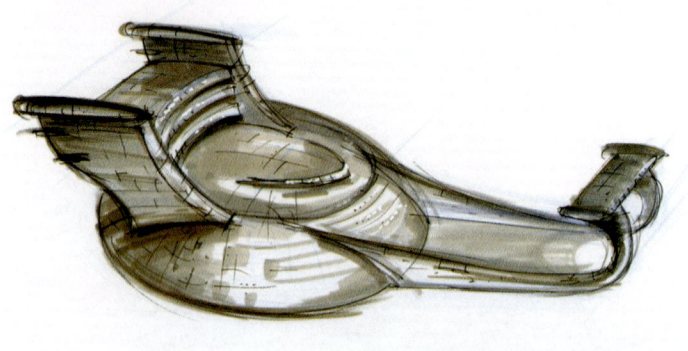

The S-1

The S-1 is modeled on how a traditional Santa sleigh might have evolved. The front of the sleigh is designed to look like upturned ski runners. We wanted the ship to feel huge, so you don't see it in a lot of wide shots. We often let it dominate the frame and early on we show it in profile so we can see the resemblance to an old fashioned sleigh silhouette.

—Alan Short, animation supervisor

S-1 Exterior

After a variety of different concepts from George Hull and other artists, Evgeni Tomov came up with the basic shape of the ship and mocked it up in 3D with Lei Chen. I took over and spent months to define it in detail. Some of the technical ideas are based on drawings from Richard Livingston. Originally from far away, the bridge looked like a much larger deck. When we talked about it, we decided the bridge had to become smaller. Finally, from far away, it was left to look as small as a dot so that the entire ship would look bigger. Underneath are panels so you don't have one smooth surface; there are thousands of hatches where elves drop out and I had to define where the hatches were and how they are arranged. I had to develop an automatic system so they didn't intersect. On the downside of S-1, if you look up, you can see that the basic structure is a snowflake.

—Till Nowak, digital set designer

Flying Through Space in 3D

We tried to play with perceived perspective on the film and just have fun with it. For example, in the opening scene where Santa first comes out onto the bridge, we want to make him dimensional but comfortable in the sense that you get the depth kids love in all the ship components and elf gadgets but it is never distracting. It's actually really fun to look around and see all this cool stuff!

In that scene, we have the camera come in and through the windshield. The 3D really shows off all the detail on the ship. We do a lot of "trickery" with our depth creation. The foreground is regular CG effects but the background is a flat-2D matte painting. We are even separating that painting into layers to give the impression that the background is far away and you can sense the depth details. If this were a live-action movie, you wouldn't see all the depth detail in the background. We want to expand out the scene and space. It's subtle but hopefully the audience will feel like the ship is really flying through the sky and perhaps they are in the ship with Santa.

—COREY TURNER, STEREOGRAPHER

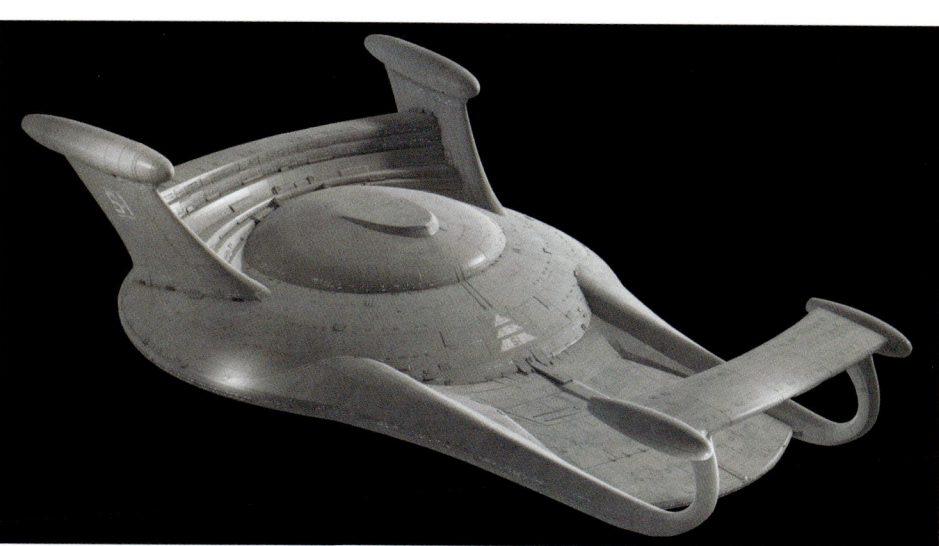

ABOVE and RIGHT: Sony Pictures Imageworks—Till Nowak.
OPPOSITE (middle): Evgeni Tomov.
OPPOSITE (below): Olivier Adam.

Aboard the S-1

Early images of the S-1 played with the idea of a giant sleigh shape. For the dock interior we looked at footage of Amazon and UPS sorting systems, and borrowed from the giant web of conveyor belts and "flippers." Till did the final design work, and to the fabulous scale and functional cool he added a range of glorious detail—mugs of cocoa in special cupholders, chairs that would ride the turbulence in a Mexican wave, an airbag, oxygen masks, an automatic red carpet for Santa.

Down in the "troop carrier" deck, a close inspection of the consoles will reveal emergency buckets of coal for exceptionally naughty children, tubes that refill the stocking guns with chocolate and candy canes, first-aid kits for dog bites and wrapping paper cuts, and of course, for the modern Health and Safety conscious elf, hand sanitizer dispensers for use between each child delivery.

—Sarah Smith, director/writer

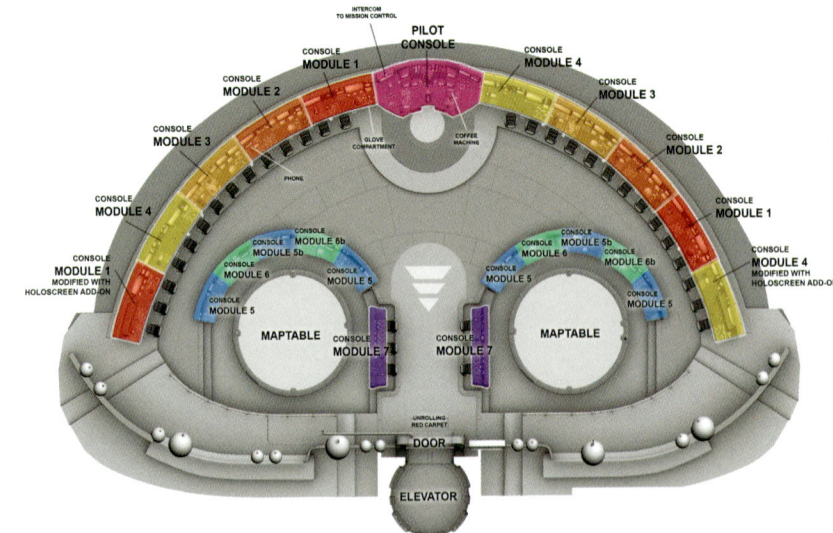

More Militaristic and Functional

The design for the bridge of the S-1 started with a shiny, white kind of *Star Trek* design. Then Sarah and Evgeni pushed me to go darker and make it more like a submarine, more militaristic and functional. Olivier Adam and Barry Cook also gave me a lot of design input. We also tried to avoid being too close to *Star Trek*. The big map tables, for example, are based on round shapes. I personally am a fan of circles so everything is based on circles, which gives it a strong, basic geometric concept and helps pull it away from being realistic.

—Till Nowak, digital set designer

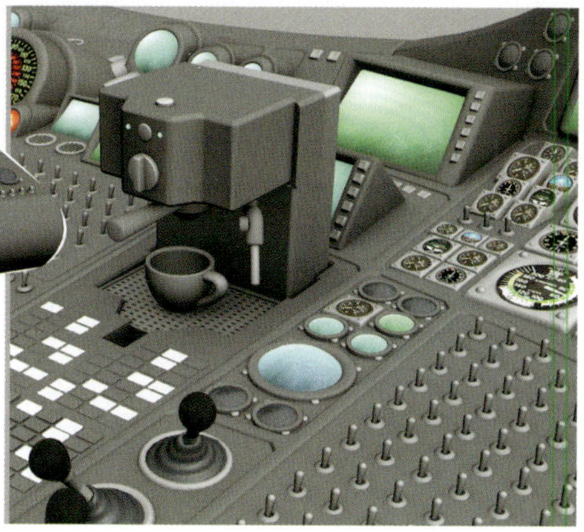

Scenes That Were Cut

We storyboarded a whole sequence where we follow Santa going into the ship, traveling all the way through it, showcasing the elves and the unique jobs they do. The scene took a lot time but had little character development, and didn't show anything we hadn't seen before.

We cut another sequence in this map room where we got to see them stacking up presents on this kind of life-sized hologram of a world map. It was a huge set piece that was fun to watch but Santa was not actually interacting with anyone so we decided to let it be background atmosphere without being highlighted.

—Donnie Long, head of story

OPPOSITE (above): Alexei Nechytaylo.
OPPOSITE (middle, left and above): Till Nowak.

The Dispatch Room

One of the most difficult times during production was the two months I spent working on the dispatch room. It was all based on ideas and drawings by Olivier Adam, our environment art director. We were trying to create the 3D grid to match the 2D ideas of our art director. I made layouts with 10 to 20 layers to create this 10-story-high room. We looked at photos and videos of conveyer belts at FedEx and other companies. We had to answer so many questions such as: Is the scanner big enough for the biggest present? If a kid gets a canoe will it go through the scanner?

—TILL NOWAK, DIGITAL SET DESIGNER

ABOVE LEFT: (all) Olivier Adam.
ABOVE: Warning signs designed by Till Nowak, Alexei Nechytaylo, and Jerry Loveland.
BELOW: Till Nowak.

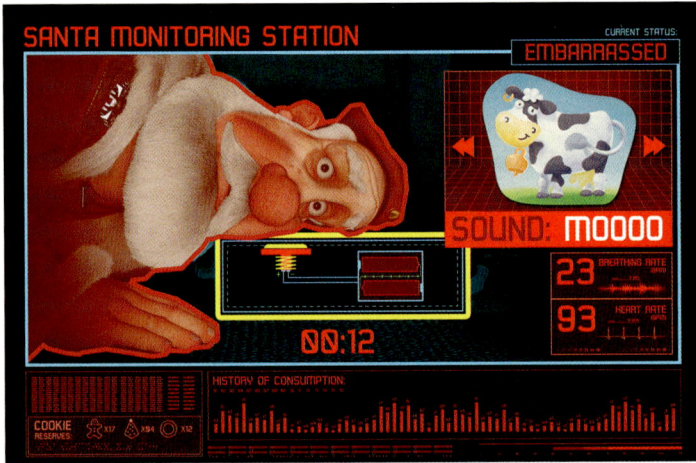

Cow Says Moo

One of the greatest and most time-consuming challenges of the movie was the thousands of screens and monitors in vision shot after shot.

Alexei Nechytaylo was the genius behind the huge task of creating an image for each of these screens. He designed an entire original North Pole operating system, from boot-up screens to file menus, task bars, screensavers and error messages. Alongside this are operational information, maps, blueprints, floor plans and Santa's current jollity rating by percentage.

Animation provided Alexei with loops, cycles and sequence specific on-screen action, news reports and numerous shots of elves making deliveries to help populate the screens.

There was a delicate balance to find between a cool, high-tech look which was funny because it took itself seriously, and something that actually looked too serious. The "Waker" sequence for example—the movie's take on a bomb-diffusing drama—initially featured very cool state-of-the-art graphics which looked amazing, yet somehow stepped on the comedy. Alexei softened the edginess of these graphics with comedic, low-fi graphics about the toy itself; the Milk Maid got her own screen and animated musical notes . . . even a cow got a caption!

—Sarah Smith, director/writer

ABOVE: Alexei Nechytaylo and Evan Parsons.

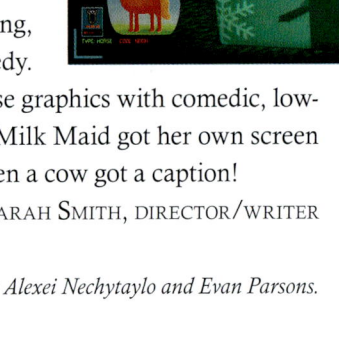

M.C.S. Santa Elf
WAKER! WE HAVE A WAKER! AND SANTA'S IN THERE!

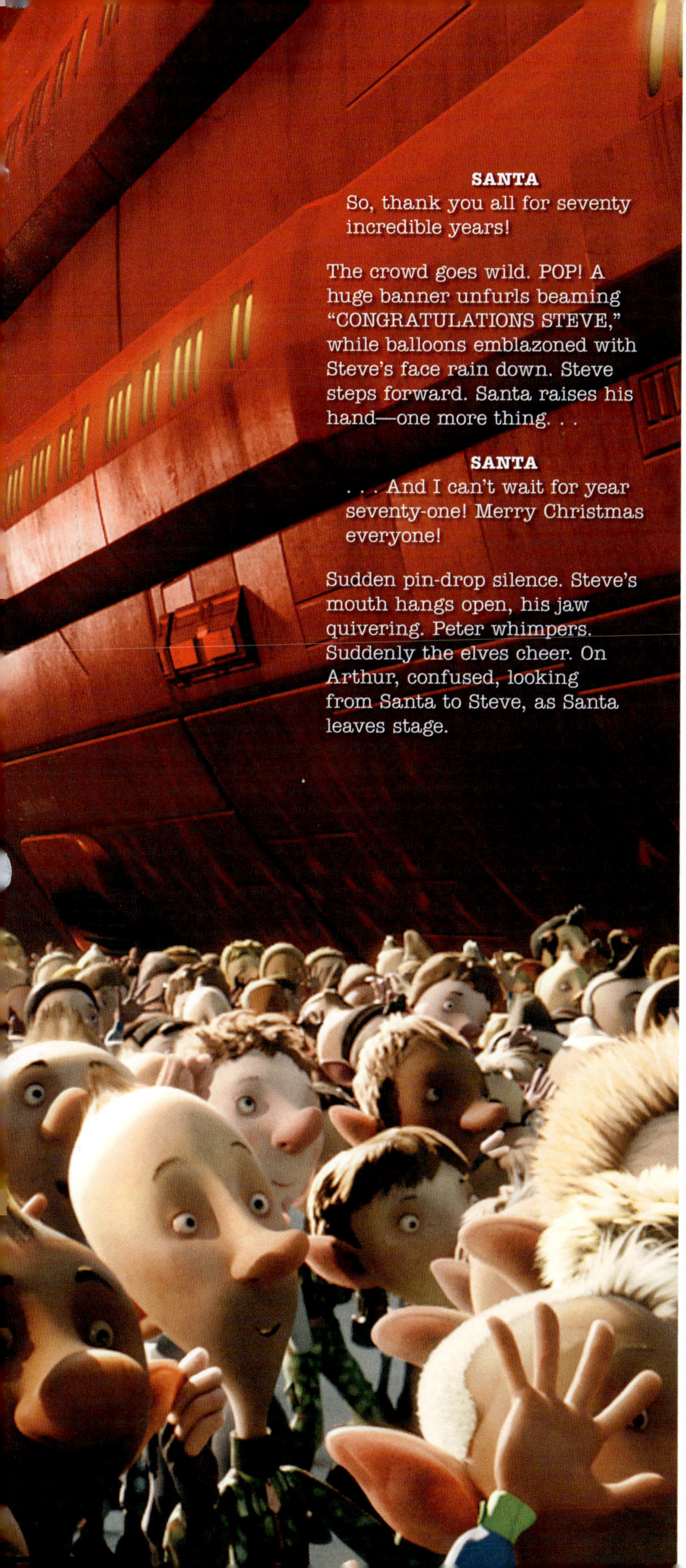

SANTA
So, thank you all for seventy incredible years!

The crowd goes wild. POP! A huge banner unfurls beaming "CONGRATULATIONS STEVE," while balloons emblazoned with Steve's face rain down. Steve steps forward. Santa raises his hand—one more thing...

SANTA
...And I can't wait for year seventy-one! Merry Christmas everyone!

Sudden pin-drop silence. Steve's mouth hangs open, his jaw quivering. Peter whimpers. Suddenly the elves cheer. On Arthur, confused, looking from Santa to Steve, as Santa leaves stage.

Mission Accomplished NOT!

The scene where Santa announces that he is not retiring after 70 years is an important beat in the emotional landscape of *Arthur Christmas*. Here we get our first hint that all is not well within the Claus family. Up until this moment, it seemed like a perfectly executed Christmas operation, but now we know that there is more going on under the surface. How will Santa's announcement impact the other characters? The stage is being set for the conflicts that will soon arise.

—Bob Osher, President, Sony Pictures Digital Productions

The Fickleness of Elves

The elves are also supposed to be a little bit like the fickle British public; one minute they are in love with the royal family and the next minute are gossiping about them. Then they love them again.

—Sarah Smith, director/writer

60,000 Elves

The elf crowds in the Mission Accomplished sequence were another challenge. One shot, mac440, had over 60,000 elves and required 6 months of processing time (if done on a single computer) to generate the simulation of all those characters.

—Stirling Duguid, CG Supervisor

ABOVE: Beat board by Adam Cootes.

119

Gwen

voiced by Romana Marquez

Risking It All for One Kid

I remember an old episode of *Star Trek* from when I was a kid. Spock and Kirk would argue about the needs of the many versus the needs of the few. And Spock would never understand why you'd risk the entire USS *Enterprise* to go back and save one man. Kirk would say, "You just don't get it. It's about life."

Arthur is like that; he would risk everything to go back for one kid. I hope kids recognize and relate to that idea.

—PETE BAYNHAM, SCREENWRITER

ABOVE RIGHT: Alexei Nechytaylo.
RIGHT: Beat board by Adam Cootes.
OPPOSITE ABOVE LEFT: Steven Hanson.
OPPOSITE ABOVE RIGHT and ABOVE: Tim Watts and Stephen Hanson.
OPPOSITE BELOW: Stephen Hanson.

Believable Environment

Arthur Christmas is unusual in that it is not heavily stylized; the feel is closer to the real world and live action than most of the animated films. The environment is very believable; our visual reference was photographs like the satellite pictures from NASA for the distant Earth shots and examples of artistic photography in general. When determining the look, color and lighting of a shot we would ask ourselves: "Can this impression be achieved with a photo camera?" Most of the layouts for the establishing shots were inspired by the work of the cinematographer Roger Deakins who uses a lot of symmetry and pattern-like visuals combining realistic elements in seemingly impossible compositions. For example, in the vista shots in the Serengeti, the first reveal of where Gwen lives in the cul-de-sac (above), the North Pole corridors or the Clauses Christmas dinner sequences, realistic elements are composed in a deliberately symmetrical way or come together in patterns that are designed, yet believable. We use handheld camera techniques in the more dynamic sequences and that is also unusual in an animated film.

—Evgeni Tomov, production designer

The Village of Trelew

My favorite set is the English village of Trelew, and we went there to take as many pictures as possible. Sarah was very keen to ensure our village had a storybook feel, but also looked real. We designed the curvy, hilly look of Cornwall, and the white-painted houses mixed with electric cables, plastic bins, wall advertising and modern streetlights. Our world is brimming with the mixed-up beauty of natural landscapes and the hugely human additions.

—Olivier Adam, environment art director

RIGHT: Early drawings by Evgeni Tomov and Olivier Adam.
OPPOSITE: Evgeni Tomov.

The World Outside the Pole

To design sets with "real" detail but graphic layouts is a simple concept. But when we venture outside into the natural and human world, the question arose of how to carry that style through. We decided to stay with our mantra—it all must feel as though "It Could Be True." We looked at photography of the earth from the air, the polar ice, Africa, etc, and picked out inspiration from the amazing images that exist of extraordinarily graphic phenomena in nature—river deltas, ice floes, tree patterns, etc.

The other problem was that we need so MUCH world. This is a road movie; there are multiple one-off sets outside the North Pole world. There was a lot of technical improvisation to make it possible to achieve so much.

The North Pole

I always wanted our Christmas film to recapture what I felt watching the 1982 Raymond Briggs animated short *The Snowman*. It contains one of the most glorious flying sequences in animation or live action, in which you feel yourself soaring over the world on a snowy Christmas night as a snowman flies with a little boy to the North Pole. It's rendered with pale drawings that give the night a feeling of light and air. After the sad dark sequence at the North Pole in which it seems all is lost and all the lights go out, we wanted a lift like that.

To capture perfect storybook compositions in a natural North Pole, we had the idea of idea of using momentary found images. We were inspired by a series of adverts for British TV's Channel 4, in which, as the camera travels as if in a car or train, elements of the environment out the window—an electricity pylon, telephone wires, a pole—appear to line up for a brief moment into a perfect replica of the Channel's "4" logo. This was the idea behind the MOON SHOT—a clump of icebergs line up into the perfect framing for the moon. The sequence has a lot of technical challenges—snow, ice, water, aurora borealis and the carving of a cloud!

—Sarah Smith, director/writer

How the Old System Works

We only see the North Pole briefly when Arthur and Grandsanta dash out of the barn on the sleigh. It's when Arthur sees how the old system works. It's a magical beautiful moment.

—Doug Ikeler, VFX supervisor

ABOVE: Laurent Ben-Mimoun.
RIGHT: Michael Kurinsky.

Toronto

I thought it would be funny if this old-fashioned sleigh crashed into the most modern, neon, contemporary city as an early obstacle. There would be no place for them to hide in the modern world. I had been to Toronto quite recently and I remembered going to the top of the CN Tower and thinking that it if you were above the clouds, it would look like a space ship.

—Pete Baynham, screenwriter

Streaky Hot Light

Toronto is our urban moment of black monolithic skyscrapers with streaky hot light. We play the whole sequence as very high contrast. They are basically trapped in a maze. It's covered in snow but at the same time it's super high contrast with bright brights and dark darks.

—Doug Ikeler, VFX supervisor

The Journey

The heart of the story is that family is the most important part of life. It's a road movie as a metaphor of life. Not like a Santa movie about gifts and magic, *Arthur Christmas* is about flawed people trying to figure out how to get along with each other. It makes it different from other Christmas movies in that it's not about the destination but the journey.

Aardman has a focus on character that a lot of studios strive for but Aardman is successful in achieving. I feel that this movie fits into the Aardman legacy because at the end of the day it's a movie about characters as opposed to being about a spectacle. Of course it deals with the world, not just a small village, but at the end of the day the emotions are very human.

My favorite scene is the Toronto sequence because, as a Canadian, I liked that Hollywood acknowledged the fact that Canada exists and people live there.

—Kris Pearn, story artist

OPPOSITE (top) Alexei Nechytaylo and Evgeni Tomov.
ABOVE: Beat board by Adam Cootes.

ARTHUR
Toronto's in CANADA!

GRANDSANTA
The Santas always come through Canada! Nobody lives here!

Flying Over Toronto

This sequence came from an idea we had that the CN tower would look like a space ship if it were isolated above clouds, and that this would be a funny thing for them to run into unexpectedly. Also, it's a relatively new city.

Again we hit the problem of how fast the sleigh is going. It's a chicken-and-egg puzzle—how fast they go determines how much city we needed them to go through, yet we want to see what the city looks like whizzing by to determine how fast we want them to go. The sequence doesn't work if it's just a blur! A Previs team laid out a city from a small number of repeating "blocks" of buildings. It was instantly clear that with a bit of judicious dressing and lighting and some building "specials" dropped in, the camera would never pick up this kind of "cheat." This was a relief because to build out a large city with many different streets in detail would have been impossibly costly for two minutes of action.

—Sarah Smith, director/writer

ABOVE: Alexei Nechytaylo.

Why Idaho?

After Toronto, they are being bashed about the world. It felt lovely to have them come down in the middle of nowhere. We toyed around with them coming down in a place where people believed in UFOs.

—Pete Baynham, screenwriter

In the Middle of Nowhere

This sequence had many incarnations. It seemed like the essential scene in a road movie—we wanted the characters horribly lost in the middle of nowhere preferably in mid-West America! We reworked the story of the scene many times—in one version Bob ended up fully wrapped by Bryony, in the boot of the sleigh, with Arthur worriedly feeding him turkey jerky through a hole!

But visually it always had the same quality. An empty *North by Northwest* plain, an *X Files* mist, and a hint of *Fargo* in the lines of perspective and the geometric patterns made by black tires lying on white snow. The house itself is the type that aliens ALWAYS decide to land near! They have a porch with a creaky rocking chair, a door that bangs in the breeze, and blinds at the window to let in spooky alien light! And it has to have one of those wind tower things you only get in America. Serves Bob right for living there!

—Sarah Smith, director/writer

What Didn't Happen in Dayton, Idaho

There are always bits you have to lose. They're like the soldiers who die in battle for the greater cause. Even if they're your finest work, they get cut in service to the story. One of my favorites involved Bob, the UFO guy with the gun. We had this idea that Grandsanta and Arthur would panic after Bob sees them. They kidnap him, throw him into the trunk of the sleigh and then fly around the world with him. Then, when they are being shot at, Bob falls out of the sleigh and, at the same point, we cut to a French woman sitting in her house writing to Santa and asking for a man. At that moment, Bob crashes through her ceiling and when the credits run, you see them as a couple. Sarah and I loved this idea but ultimately, it all became too complicated and strayed too far away from the core characters so it had to go.

—Pete Baynham, screenwriter

Idaho

Cut to reveal the full crazy picture. Arthur, hood up, face a patchy red from his snow allergy, is balanced precariously on the roof of a remote tractor dealership, trying to take the big metal deer which forms its logo. Something gives, he slips noisily knocking out a light.

GRANDSANTA (*looks around*)
Maybe we pulled to the right a bit, we're a reindeer short. France!
(*climbs down, hobble off the sleigh*)
BONJOUR! OU EST LE BOULANGERIE?

Africa

Why Africa?

Due to a navigational error, Arthur and Grandsanta wind up in the Serengeti. Part of the comedy is that they land in a wildlife park. The choice of places where they land is not really random, it is plot driven. We asked ourselves, if things went really wrong, where would they wind up?

—David Sproxton, producer, Co-founder of Aardman

We came up with the idea of them landing in Africa pretty early on in writing the script. That just felt like a really funny idea—to have Santa and his sleigh on the Serengeti surrounded by African wildlife. I have not seen that in any Christmas film. From there, the more they go wrong, the more they go wrong. It's an ever-widening circle as they get further and further away from where they need to be. And the clock is ticking away in real time towards dawn in the UK.

—Pete Baynham, screenwriter

Sun and Moon

We wanted Africa to feel hot, a place of danger and the opposite of the snowy Christmas world. That's not easy when the sun isn't out. So we had the idea of a huge blood moon.

—Sarah Smith, director/writer

ABOVE: Evgeni Tomov.

Golden Tones of Africa

Each location in the film has its own theme and color palate. In Africa we use golden tones and warm lights that set the place apart from the other locations which are mostly set in winter snow. This environment is designed to look hot and warm, even at night. Lots of dust gets kicked up, showing how dry it is. We worked with violets, yellows and vivid red.

—Doug Ikeler, VFX supervisor

The Serengeti Look

For Serengeti, I tried to play with an African and simple graphic pattern based on dots: using tufts of grass and the typical "umbrella" trees look and linearity, and strips of tall yellowish grass alternately with strips of red soil.

—Olivier Adam, environment art director

Convincingly Believable

The colors in the Serengeti scene seem somewhat exaggerated but they actually do not stray too far from photos of the place. We don't have a lot of purple, pink or any vinyl and synthetic colors in our palette. Ours are the colors that can be achieved with a real camera. A lot of animated films have their own stylized color palette with garish colors that don't appear in real life, while we tried not to make our world look artificially colored but rather convincingly believable.

—Evgeni Tomov, production designer

Imperfect Double Action

We tried to enhance the live-action feel of the film with the editing. We wanted to make some imperfect double-action cuts, which is not something usually done in animated films. These scenes were mapped out in boards and handed over to the pre-viz team, who strung together shots from different angles to give us coverage. These rushes enabled us to cut the footage in a similar way to live action. In the Serengeti, for example, the camera feels like it has a hand-held quality to it—long sections were animated and then an operated camera was applied to the shots to provide rushes to edit with, as you would in a live-action environment.

—James Cooper, editor

There were over 130 character, vehicle and prop rigs created for the film. From lions to sleighs to elves to our main character Arthur, this was Imageworks' most complex character movie to date.

—Aaron Pfau, Character Set-up Supervisor

ABOVE: Beat board by Adam Cootes.

ERNIE
You can't rush the Signalator. Got to play 'er gentle, like a woman.

Mexico: The Wrong Trelew

An "Aha!" Moment

Mexico is an "aha!" moment in the movie. You think Arthur is going to deliver the gift to Gwen. So the first half of the sequence is nondescript but kind of dark and eerie. You want to set up to the viewer that something is not quite right but, at the same time, everything is normal. After Arthur realizes that he's in the wrong place, then it's all about wrong colors. We have the neon signs, bright greens, red, and purples. As he is being chased, you see that everything is wrong for both Christmas and England. It's a chaotic, agitated moment so the colors go off the charts and the palate gets plain crazy.

—Doug Ikeler, VFX supervisor

ABOVE: Beat board by Adam Cootes.

Intruding

This is one of the first sequences when Arthur realizes he has to take more responsibility for what is happening. Grandsanta refuses to deliver the gift, so Arthur has to go into this house. It's creepy to walk into someone's house. Even though there is a sense of Christmas with the tree and decorations, there is a feeling that he is intruding. Then he discovers there already is a bike under the tree. That pops the balloon and we play the rest for comedy. I love the idea that the scene is really loaded toward the idea of what it would really be like to be Santa and would you want to do this job. We tried to set up the idea that Arthur is not yet ready to be Santa. The whole scene should feel wrong to him and the audience.

—Kris Pearn, story artist

Cayo de Confites, Cuba

6:48 A.M. Cayo de Confites, Cuba. Number of sleighs: 0.

On the Beach

We thought there should come a point in the story when they lose the sleigh. Sarah is a big fan of the "Now get out of that" moment in a film. So this is the ultimate of that for them. They lose the sleigh and they have like 47 minutes until the sun rises in Trelew. At this point, we wanted them to be somewhere on the wrong side of the Atlantic. We put them on a real island in Cuba and there is literally nothing there. It's probably the least Christmassy part of the world. That seemed like fun.

—Pete Baynham, screenwriter

Lowest Emotional Point

The beach scene is the lowest emotional point in the movie but delicate and subtle. Arthur is disillusioned, so the colors are monochromatic. Here is an intimate, soul-searching conversation between Arthur and Grandsanta. It is the saddest scene in the movie until Arthur gets his mojo back.

—Evgeni Tomov, production designer

Arthur Loses Faith

The beach scene is where Arthur loses faith; everything builds to this moment when he realizes that Santa does not exist. For Arthur, this knocks out his belief system. It's like finding out your parents were on the wrong side of the war. Your dad isn't a superhero; he messed up. This is the point where you realize your parents are human, which is always a painful thing (more painful for Arthur because his dad is also Santa Claus).

Arthur has a choice here: he can give up on Christmas and give up on his family, or he can finish the mission. Ironically, it's the idea of Christmas that hurts him and it's also the idea of Christmas that brings him back into the movie. Arthur is a very empathetic person, which is what he clings to when he realizes that Gwen won't get her gift. He may have lost faith, but he's still a good guy. He's still awkward, he hasn't successfully Rambo'd up yet—in the next scene he tries to row a boat to England—but at least he is not banging into his choices. He is making them for himself. He started this whole adventure by accident—he never wanted to be on that sleigh with Grandsanta. But this scene is the first moment that Arthur, as a motivated hero, makes the choice to do the right thing for the right reason.

—Kris Pearn, story artist

ABOVE: Olivier Adam.

Atlantic

Rowing Across the Ocean

The mood changes after the beach scene, so there is more contrast, more action. The color palette changes from the melancholic greenish blue-gray into steely cold blue and the increased contrast gives the sequence a dramatic feel that is supportive of the story. The changed, now stormier clouds in the sky help convey that as well. You get the sense of the overpowering scale of the ocean and the challenge of being in this tiny boat trying to row across it.

—Evgeni Tomov, production designer

Arthur's Determination

When we first conceived of losing the sleigh, we loved the heroism of Arthur just keeping on walking until he hit the ocean, when he would start trying to row to England with only half an hour to go till sunrise. It was the ultimate proof of determination.

—Sarah Smith, director/writer

Comedic Rat-a-tat

Here Arthur solves his problem with worry which is a concept I think is so funny. I like the juxtaposition between the physical action of Arthur hurdling around at mach three on the sleigh trying to run the gauntlet over sweaty, heaving deer with the silence of cutting to Grandsanta and Bryony in the row boat. I feel there's a nice comedic rat-a-tat in that scene, which is always fun to watch.

—Kris Pearn, story artist

OPPOSITE: Lighting paintovers by Michael Kurinsky.
ABOVE: Evgeni Tomov.

UNFITA

UNFITA

The UNFITA scene is one of the last ones I worked on. It consisted of two rooms. The control room is like a smaller version of Steve's Mission Control. My interpretation was to make it more realistic in terms of sizes and the devices that are shown. It's more edgy and lacks the magic of the North Pole. This set more represents our daily life on earth and while the other, the North Pole, is our imagination.

—Till Nowak, digital set designer

ABOVE: Evgeni Tomov and Dark Hoffman.
LEFT: Alexei Nechytaylo.
RIGHT: Early concept drawings by Peter de Sève.
BELOW: Sergio Casa Castano, Bjorn-Erik Aschim.

Elinora Da Silva
voiced by Eva Longoria

Nobody wants to be got out of bed in the early hours of Christmas morning to deal with a global crisis. Mrs. Da Silva, Secretary General of The United Northern Federal International Treaty Alliance (UNFITA), faces an unenviable dilemma: what to do about a strange red craft zipping around the globe at incredible speed, leaving a trail of destruction before going into orbit. And what to make of an operative's response to her command to target the propulsion system of what we know to be a battered sleigh being pulled by an ancient reindeer: "Ma'am, it doesn't have any. The engine appears to be . . . furry."

ABOVE: Early concept drawings by Peter de Sève.

Upside Down at 1,000 MPH

There are cheats in any action sequence. If you have to sell the audience on the "fact" that reindeer can fly, then within that world you have to also portray believable physics. When Arthur is traveling upside down at a 1,000 miles an hour, we borrow from real world physics and try to make it believable. We don't want to sell the audience short.

—ALAN SHORT, ANIMATION SUPERVISOR

RIGHT: *Evgeni Tomov.*

3D Aware

The movie was designed in what I call "3D aware." We encourage the animators to not cheat the perspective or go for the "in your face" gags. We just want them to be aware of what can happen in 3D. The real obvious 3D gags can look good on a sizzle reel but in the movie it tends to pull people out of the story.

—Chris Juen, co-producer

Too Militaristic

Towards the end there were threats that were deemed too militaristic and destructive. We had fighter jets, tanks and whole armies mobilizing to chase the sleigh. We decided this was too much of a real world threat and the huge scale of the military operation threatened the anonymity of Christmas. The military thinks they're chasing an alien ship, so they want to keep it quiet, and Arthur wants to keep the sleigh from being seen, so both sides are trying to discreetly win over the other. We realized that the way technology flies today, if the military were to engage the sleigh, everyone would know about it. So how do we show that struggle without people asking logic questions? We decided to keep most of the action in the air away from the town, so it seemed credible that no one noticed the action in the sky.

—Donnie Long, head of story

MRS SANTA

Trelew's on course of 187.7 degrees from the geographic pole, but as it's the old sleigh we should allow a drift margin of 1,000 miles either side of the Greenwich meridian.

(*shows items prepared*)

I've got a sweater for Arthur, your father's pills and some nice sweet tea.

Space

The interesting thing about outer space is that very few of us have seen it; we have only seen pictures of it. There are far more stars visible than we are used to seeing in photos of the earth from space, because of the exposures used. So when we first looked at realistic imagery for this sequence, showing glittering star-studded blackness, it seemed wrong. So we chose to show space as we have seen it in space photographs, movies, sci-fi shows and shuttle re-entry footage, etc. In this case we replaced truth and reality with what people imagine to be true.

On the other hand, the startling image of the sun rising round the edge of the earth casting a line of light across it is entirely truthful, and very beautiful.

—Sarah Smith, director/writer

ABOVE: *Beat board by Adam Cootes.*
BELOW: *Lighting Key by Evgeni Tomov.*

LEGAL WAIVER

I, CLIENT 477858HK, hereby acknowledge receipt of this GLAMOURFAST ULTRA X-3 within the WINDOW OF CHRISTMAS. I surrender all rights against THE NORTH POLE in perpetuity and throughout the universe. I agree to TOTAL CONFIDENTIALITY in all matters including, but not limited to, SANTA, SANTA'S FAMILY, NORTH POLE PERSONNEL and any and all STATISTICAL ANOMALIES.

I acknowledge that delivering SO MANY GIFTS in one night is REALLY HARD and NOBODY'S PERFECT.

I agree to hold ALL INFORMATION in strict confidence and to disclose same to NOBODY, ESPECIALLY CHILDREN (under CLIENT 477858HK's own blanket or specific agreement form) to protect and preserve the confidentiality of such disclosures and who are designated by CLIENT 477858HK to evaluate the CONFIDENTIAL INFORMATION for the aforementioned purposes.

The NORTH POLE may contact me about new goods, promotions or services.

Please Sign Below:

ABOVE: In this scene Steve arrives at the wrong Trelew and asks Pedro to sign a waiver of confidentiality. The document is only on screen for a few seconds but in keeping with the attention to detail that was the focus of every moment in the film, Pete Baynham wrote an actual contract. BELOW: Lighting Key by Michael Kurinsky and Evgeni Tomov.

STEVE
You wouldn't mind signing a legal waiver...

Gwen Hines' Trelew, Including The 1,000-Yard Dash

Gangly Bloke on a Bike

The sequence in which Arthur cycles through Trelew was known to us as the "Thousand Yard-Dash." It was our joke on *The Incredibles*' Thousand-Mile Dash. They have an amazingly complex, fast-moving action chase with giant robots; we have a gangly bloke trying to ride a tiny kid's bike while it's being wrapped. He may only have to go a thousand yards but it's just as hard!

—Sarah Smith, director/writer

Because of all the preparation for this scene, Alan [Hawkins] choreographed exactly where each piece of paper was for every shot, where each part of the bike got wrapped, where the tape would be placed and where Bryony's hands would be at any given moment. Even with the cheats, we made it believable within our world. We never went for the cartoony thing of making all the action a blur with hands and feet coming out of a cloud of dust. We didn't want to cheat the audience. We wanted to create a world where all of this was possible.

—Alan Short, animation supervisor

That's a Wrap

Paper is used in a handful of previous scenes but used the most here. Paper in general is a difficult material to animate. We didn't create a special program for it so it fell on the animators to make it work. A piece of paper goes from being very flat when you unroll it to crinkling and folding and all its edges have to be introduced. This is very difficult to accomplish especially when you are also planning and choreographing a series of actions through the sequence.

—Alan Hawkins, animation lead

RIGHT: Lighting Keys by Evgeni Tomov.

Cold Winter Morning and Hot Sunlight

Once we are in Trelew at the end of the film, the first glimpse of the sun is not welcoming, although still beautiful. We used more saturated colors for the sunlight to establish the danger of the sunrise to our heroes' mission. After a few fairly monochromatic but dramatic sequences, in Arthur's last dash to Gwen's house we periodically introduce a hot saturated color of the light to maintain the tension of the scene. The strong contrast in the color temperature—cold winter morning shadows and hot sunlight—is intended to enhance the drama in this part of the movie.

—Evgeni Tomov, Production Designer